Arrian: Per

ARRIAN

PERIPLUS PONTI EUXINI

Edited with Introduction, Translation
and Commentary by

Aidan Liddle

Bristol Classical Press

First published in 2003 by
Bristol Classical Press
an imprint of
Gerald Duckworth & Co. Ltd.
90-93 Cowcross Street, London EC1M 6BF
Tel: 020 7490 7300
Fax: 020 7490 0080
inquiries@duckworth-publishers.co.uk
www.ducknet.co.uk

A catalogue record for this book is available
from the British Library

ISBN 1 85399 661 0

Typeset by Aidan Dodson
Printed and bound in Great Britain by
Biddles Ltd, *www.biddles.co.uk*

Contents

Preface

It has been almost 200 years since an English translation of Arrian's *Periplus Ponti Euxini* was last published. This new edition, I hope, will bring it to a new audience who have yet to discover this fascinating little work. It is not intended to be a thorough critical edition – others have done that better than I could hope to – but an introduction to the various themes and subjects Arrian touched upon in writing it.

Although its significance is much broader than topography, it is inevitable that a commentary on this work will involve a lot of names. In general, I have hellenised the names of Greek people and places. Rules are there to be broken, however, and I have done so wherever I felt that the Latinised or Anglicised form of a name would be more familiar, or at least less confusing (such as Aeschylus, Byzantium, Jason).

In order to help the reader find his or her way around the work, there are two maps at the end of the book. They should be sufficient for general orientation: those with an interest in the topography of the Black Sea, however, should turn to the excellent *Barrington Atlas of the Greek and Roman*

World, grid references to which are included in the Commentary.

My thanks are due to John Betts, formerly of the Bristol Classical Press, and Deborah Blake of Duckworth, for their faith in this project; to the BCP's anonymous reader, who made some very helpful comments at an early stage; to Ray Davies and Gareth Cheeseman, for technical help, especially with the maps; to Christopher Liddle, for his proof-reading skills (the doubtless myriad errors and solecisms still remaining are, of course, my own responsibility); and to my friends and family for their unfailing encouragement. But above all, I am indebted to Nicholas Purcell, without whom this book would never have been thought of, let alone written.

A.T.L.
London, June 2003

Introduction

The Black Sea is a strange and distant place, a place
of witches and heroes, a place where the water can
be both salt and fresh, a place of captive giants and
ferocious tribes. From earliest Greek mythology its
farther shores have been the locale of 'otherness', the
natural residence of all that was out of place in the
Mediterranean world, yet inextricably linked to it.
Plato was unusual in seeing the pond around which
the peoples of the world sat like frogs as comprising
the entire body of water east of the Pillars of
Hercules:[1] for most ancient – and many modern –
writers, the Black Sea is a foreign sea, barely a sea
at all, and separate from the arena of civilised
human transactions.

It should be no surprise, then, that it has been the
inspiration for numerous strange works of literature,
including that which concerns us here. To Arrian of
Nicomedia the Euxine Sea was indeed that place of
myth and legend. But it was also a place of history,
political intrigue, and a place that concerned him
directly: not only had he grown up along its
seaboard, but he returned as a statesman and soldier
at the peak of his public career to govern its most
important province. The work that this sea inspired,

the *Circumnavigation of the Black Sea*, or *Periplus
Ponti Euxini*, is a strange and disparate work – part
military and diplomatic report, part fantastic
mythological guidebook, part friendly private
correspondence – and as such has often been
overlooked, at least in English. Yet it is more than a
literary curiosity. It sheds much light upon an
important, yet obscure, corner of the Roman frontier;
it illuminates the contemporary image of the
emperor Hadrian, one of the most elusive men ever
to have ascended to the purple; and it stands almost
alone as a record of the activity of the governor of
this important province. Above all, it is a product of
its times, and its author, as revealed in its pages,
supremely representative of them.

This introductory essay will attempt both to treat
the major themes in culture and history that form
the background to Arrian, his career (the
culmination of which, and the immediate inspiration
of this opuscule, was his governorship of
Cappadocia), and the *Periplus Ponti Euxini* itself,
and to address more specific questions, such as those
of authenticity and textual tradition. It will also
relate the seemingly disparate aspects of the
Periplus to its complex political and cultural world.
But it is to Arrian the man that we shall first turn
our attention.

1 Arrian's career

The task of unravelling Arrian's life and career has
long exercised scholarly minds. While certain

significant details consistently evade confirmation, fragments of inscriptions, notices in contemporary and later writings, and the internal evidence of his own works make the general outline of his life reasonably clear.[2]

L. Flavius Arrianus Xenophon[3] was born in the city of Nicomedia, the capital of the Asian province of Bithynia. The name demonstrates his Roman citizenship, which was evidently of long standing: Syme has suggested that the L. Flavius who made the initial grant to Arrian's ancestors was the suffect consul of 33 BC, who was then with Antony in the East. Arrian's family, then, was part of the old aristocracy of Bithynia; but in terms of the Roman hierarchy it was a provincial member of the Equestrian Order. Arrian was certainly the first of that family to attain the *fasces* of the consulship, and it would appear too that he was the first to be adlected to the Senate.[4]

The year of his birth is unknown; by working back from the date of his consulship, which is assigned to either 129 or 130 (of which more below), AD 86 is conventionally assumed. The next landmark in the young man's development is his studies with the Stoic Epictetus at Nicopolis in north-western Greece, towards the end of the first decade of the second century.[5] This period left a great impression upon Arrian, and it is then that he may have first met the future emperor Hadrian, who also visited the philosopher.[6] A further link to the young Hadrian is provided by C. Avidius Nigrinus (suffect consul for 110), on whose *consilium* as *legatus Augusti pro*

praetore for Achaea Arrian is attested around 111-
114. Nigrinus, a close friend of Hadrian's, would
surely have played host to the future emperor when
he was elected archon at Athens in 112.

The period between Arrian's service on the
consilium of the governor of Achaea and Hadrian's
accession in 117 is obscure. If an equestrian
background for Arrian is correct, the most likely
proposition would be a spell of service in the *militia
equestris*; it has been suggested that his claim to
have seen the rivers Inn and Save at first hand
originated in this connection,[7] and Stadter asserts
that there is 'little reason to doubt' that he served in
some capacity with Trajan in Parthia.[8] Whatever the
details of this quinquennium, it seems that Arrian's
adlection to the Senate, probably *inter praetorios*,
followed soon after his friend's accession.

The next glimmer of evidence is an inscription from
Cordoba, in the Spanish province of Baetica, in
which a proconsul named Arrianus dedicates a Greek
poem to Artemis, goddess of hunting.[9]   Further
evidence is often recognised in an apparently first-
hand account in the *Anabasis* of rites in honour of
Herakles at Tartessus in that province.[10] Nothing is
certain, however, until the suffect consulship held
with one Severus in 129 or 130.

The approximate date of Arrian's assumption of the
nominally supreme office of the *cursus honorum* is
furnished by the consular dating formula on brick
stamps found in Ostia in buildings which can be
fixed to the years 125-130.[11] The consuls for 127 and
128 are known: 129 and 130 are the gaps most likely

to be plugged by Arrian, and Syme prefers 129 on the basis that consulars often undertook an administrative appointment in Rome before taking up a post abroad.[12] That overseas command, which, for Arrian, was as governor of Cappadocia, forms the background and the *raison d'être* of the *Periplus*: as such, it deserves special consideration.

Cappadocia and the 'Pontic limes'

The province Arrian arrived to govern in about 131 had emerged from Vespasian's major reorganisation of the Eastern frontier provinces in AD 72, in which the province of Galatia was incorporated into the former Cappadocia.[13] In addition to the large swathe of central Anatolia under his immediate jurisdiction, the governor of the new province also acquired responsibility for the frontier regions of Armenia Minor and the Caucasus mountains, annexed, with the rump of the kingdom of Pontus, by Nero.

The major factor in this reorganisation was perhaps the wish to simplify and formalise the defences against the Parthians through more-or-less permanent frontier installations, as Vespasian and Titus were also doing along the Rhine and Danube: now two Roman armies policed the border, one (XII Fulminata at Melitene) facing the Parthians from Syria, the other (XV Apollinaris at Satala) the buffer state of Armenia Minor — so often the pawn in the power games of the two great empires — from Cappadocia. Consolidating this new frontier structure, Titus created a *limes* (an integrated

frontier military route) from the military port of
Trapezous on the Black Sea, base of the Black Sea
fleet or *Classis Pontica*,[14] via the legionary fortresses
of Melitene, Satala and Samosata on the upper
Euphrates, to Antioch in Syria.

The Black Sea end of this military road was vital
for trade – more specifically, the corn supply from
the north Black Sea coast, which came through
Trapezous to the armies of the Cappadocian and
Syrian frontiers; indeed, Tacitus tells us of Corbulo's
fears in 68 that hostile forces could cut supplies to
the Roman armies in Armenia Minor.[15]   But the
route was also threatened by piracy in the Black Sea
itself, and this appears to have been the primary rôle
of the Roman presence in the region, the first reason
for a supplementary 'Pontic *limes*' protecting the
flank of the Cappadocian frontier.[16] Strabo mentions
that the local kings of Colchis, a small enclave within
the mountains like a theatre leading down to the
Black Sea, had an important rôle to play in the
regulation of this activity, and it has been further
suggested that Nero's annexation in 64 of the
territory of King Polemo II of Pontus (under whose
auspices Colchis was ruled) was a direct result of
that king's failure adequately to discharge this
duty.[17]   It is no accident, then, that Arrian found
himself some seventy years later inspecting the
military installations of the coast of this small
lowland kingdom as one of his first duties as the man
in charge of a central plank of Rome's eastern
frontier.

Owing to its position, nestled in the angle formed by the eastern spur of the Pontine mountains to the south and the Caucasus mountains running diagonally from the north to the east, and easily accessible only from the sea, Colchis had always been part of the Greek, and then the Roman sphere of influence, unlike the transcaucasian kingdoms of Iberia and Albania further to the east. The first contact was made with the Greek world in the Achaean period: it was linked with the stories of the Argonauts, and was mentioned by Homer.[18] Colonies were founded on its coast by the sixth century BC; by the fifth century Athenian wine, pottery and olive oil regularly found their way to the trading stations of the Colchian coast, though – coinage aside[19] – there is no evidence for any significant degree of hellenisation. Trade continued throughout the Hellenistic period, although Alexander himself bypassed the region.

After the Romans' first intervention in the 60s BC, when Pompey pursued his arch-adversary Mithridates there, Colchis came into the sphere of the eastern portion of the kingdom of Pontus left after the Roman annexation of the western portion of it, as part of the network of 'client-kings' that supplemented direct Roman administration of its territory.[20] By AD 64, this system had clearly broken down. This was perhaps symptomatic of a wider malaise in the region: we are told by Tacitus that Nero was sending his new legion I Italica '... to the Caspian Gates and the war which he was contemplating against the Albanians' at the time of his downfall in 68, and by the Elder Pliny a decade later that Dioskourias (for Strabo in the Augustan period a flourishing trading post) was *nunc deserta*.[21] In the meantime, the civil war of 69 had reached the Black Sea: a certain Anicetus had intervened for Vitellius against Vespasian, hijacking the fleet, stirring up local tribes, and sacking Trapezous.[22]

It is hardly surprising, then, that securing Roman control over this stretch of coastline in the eastern Black Sea was a priority for emperors both before and after the civil wars. Yet this string of forts from Trapezous to Dioskourias did not just look outwards over the sea. Although Roman cultural influence was extremely low-level in the interior of the country, some measure of control in the hinterland – over movement, at least – was also important to Roman interests. This was most effectively achieved, not by military outposts beyond the zone of immediate Roman control, as in Germany beyond the Rhine after AD 9, but by these self-same coastal installations. The interior of Colchis, below the foothills of the mountain districts that hemmed the territory in and bound it to the sea, was (and in many parts still is) wet and low-lying, and covered with thick forests that made travel across the interior very difficult.[23] The sea, and the navigable rivers that penetrated the interior, were thus vital to Roman interests.

Clearly, the sea and coastal strip, though on the geographical periphery of Colchis, were vital. Transport by sea and the many navigable rivers was so easy – all the more so from the perspective of a

power that could hope to maintain control of the sea
– that these areas represented the centre of Roman
interests in the region.[24]

It is thus no coincidence that the one of the most
important forts, at Phasis, was at the head of the
region's largest river – the valley of which to this day
provides the principal means of communication with
the interior of what is now Georgia – nor that one of
Arrian's first concerns was to record whether each
river was navigable or not.

The limited military presence on this coast, though,
could not by itself secure this troublesome interior.
Military control was supplemented, as elsewhere
across the fringes of the Roman world, by a network
of client kings. Arrian's inspection was thus not
restricted to military affairs: his detailed list of tribes
and kings (*Peripl.* 11) – singling out those who had
displayed their vassalage to Rome by accepting their
crown from the hand of the emperor – demonstrates
the importance of this aspect of the Roman frontier
structure.[25]

This measure of control over the interior was
important to the second reason for the Roman
presence in Pontus, which was to keep an eye on, if
not to contain, the unpredictable tribes of the
Caucasus and beyond – chief amongst which were
the kingdoms of Iberia, in the mountainous interior,
and Albania, in the low-lying areas towards the
Caspian Sea. A stable Caucasus was invaluable for
Trajan when launching his attack on neighbouring
Armenia in 114, and Iberia was particularly
important for its control of the road south from the

Darial Pass, which crossed the otherwise impenetrable Caucasus about halfway along its length. Iberia had long been regarded as a client state (though this label applied elsewhere masks a multitude of varying realities): epigraphical evidence attests the presence, in Vespasian's reign, of Roman army units constructing a fortification at Harmozica, near modern Tblisi, ostensibly for the benefit of king Mithridates.[26] But by the time Hadrian visited the region in 129, the relationship was rocky: when he convened a meeting with various local rulers, King Pharasmenes of Iberia sent him an arrogant refusal.[27] Although it seems that relations were more cordial towards the end of Hadrian's reign,[28] the episode indicates the fine balance that operated in the region: as we hear from the *Periplus* (11.2), Pharasmenes had vassals of his own on the Black Sea coast, and may even have had ambitions in Colchis itself.[29]

The reconciliation may not have come about exclusively through diplomatic channels. The great fortress at Apsaros, as described by Arrian (*Peripl.* 6.1-3), staffed with fully five cohorts of Roman arms, commanded a crucial strategic position from which to threaten Iberia, as well as to defend the coastal route from Colchis into Cappadocia itself. Speidel believes this to be Hadrian's answer to Pharasmenes' snub, and proposes that Arrian's γνώμη to his emperor concerning the cohorts – contained in and lost with the official report, in Latin, of the inspection that Arrian submitted alongside the *Periplus*[30] – was part of the strategic thinking Hadrian was engaged upon

at that time, although Braund argues that there is
nothing in the *Periplus* to suggest that relations were
still frosty even in 132.[31] But Iberia's centrality to
the stability of the region was amply demonstrated
in 135, when Pharasmenes apparently opened the
Darial Pass to the marauding Alanoi, who swept
through Albania and Media, and would have done
serious damage in Cappadocia had Arrian not
promptly deterred them.[32] Speidel's suggestion that
Arrian was operating from Apsaros, thereby
protecting both Cappadocia and Colchis, and
menacing the barbarians' line of retreat, is
attractive.[33] Whatever the original strategic
intention in posting a garrison at Apsaros (and
indeed the other places along the coast), the fort
proved a vital part of what has been called the
Caucasian *limes.*

The coast that ran from Trapezous to the Caucasus
mountains to the north of Colchis was, then, a vital
peg in the structure of Roman domination of the east.
The *Classis Pontica* secured the east Black Sea
region, control of which was necessary for successful
manoeuvres in the area for Roman and barbarian
alike (as Anicetus proved in 68, and the Scythians in
the invasion of 250),[34] and protected the corn supply
from the northern shores of the Black Sea to
Trapezous and on to the frontier. The littoral forts
secured the safety of the coast for these operations,
and further provided a foothold for Roman dealings
with the nominally client kings of the transcaucasian
kingdoms. The maintenance of the Roman presence
– and of its influence – in this important region was

a central duty of Arrian's task as governor of
Cappadocia, the discharge of which forms the basis of
the tour described in the first part of the *Periplus*.

*

The limit of Arrian's tenure of Cappadocia is
provided both by an inscription of 137
commemorating the twentieth anniversary of
Hadrian's accession and naming Arrian as the
incumbent governor, and by a document that attests
Arrian's successor in office before Hadrian's death in
July 138.[35]   This would appear to be the end of
Arrian's career in the Roman *cursus*; although it has
been suggested that he emulated other holders of the
Cappadocian command and went on to govern Syria,
this remains no more than a possibility. The same
can be said for a subsequent proconsular
appointment, although the records for both Asia and
Africa are vacant for the year 143/4, when Arrian
would have become eligible.[36] The only evidence we
have for Arrian's public life after 137 is an
inscription naming him as *archon* at Athens for the
year 145/6, and, as Stadter points out,[37] this will
have been followed by a seat on the Areopagus, by
this time the ruling council of the city. Suggestions
that Arrian's apparently comfortable and respectable
retirement to Athens was due to a fall from imperial
favour – either that of Hadrian or of his successor,
Antoninus Pius – are unnecessary: a six-year
command in Cappadocia was in any case
extraordinary, and a long and leisured retreat from

the public life of the Empire can equally well be perceived to be a reward as a rebuke.[38] How long his retirement proved to be is strictly a matter for speculation.

2 Arrian's literary achievement

It is clear that by the time he settled in Athens the former general and statesman was celebrated for his literary achievements as much as, if not more than, for his public career. Already in the 140s, the libraries of Herodes Atticus and Rusticus, tutor to the future emperor Marcus Aurelius, contained copies of his *Diatribae*, or notes on the lectures of Epictetus, and a statue erected to him in Athens bore an inscription to 'L. Flavius Arrianus, consular, philosopher'.[39] The late ancient biographers of Arrian went so far as to suggest that he was awarded his consulship on account of the distinction of his scholarship,[40] and his younger contemporary Lucian summed him up in a memorable phrase:

καὶ Ἀρριανὸς γὰρ ὁ τοῦ Ἐπικτήτου μαθητὴς ἀνὴρ
Ῥωμαῖος ἐν τοῖς πρώτοις καὶ παιδείᾳ παρ᾽ ὅλον τὸν
βίον συγγενόμενος.[a]

Arrian himself supports this proposition, that his life had been spent in the pursuit of learning (as well as military matters, and hunting), in the

---

[a] Lucian, *Alexander* 2: 'For Arrian, the disciple of Epictetus, was one of the foremost Romans, and lived his whole life with learning'.

Cynegeticus, and again in the *Anabasis*.[41] It is now generally accepted that this reputation was firmly cemented early in Arrian's career – this in opposition to Schwartz's assertion, for long orthodox, that the bulk of his work was composed in the leisure of his retirement, and that the Cappadocian works (the *Periplus*, *Ectaxis*, and *Tactics*) represented tentative first essays.[42] Literary ambition is of course perfectly compatible with a public career – the examples of Cicero and the elder Pliny illustrate this – and it seems that the famous complaint of the latter's nephew that his post at the *aerarium Saturni* left him little time for literary pursuits, swamped as he was with *inlitteratissimae litterae*, is too often remembered at the expense of the same writer's praise of his uncle for so successfully combining high office with copious composition.[43] The *Periplus* and *Tactics*, rather, are mature essays, delivered to an audience already familiar with his work – a close inspection of the *Periplus* alone, as will become apparent, reveals a depth of sophistication and an ambition in the work surely beyond a first literary attempt.

If his reputation in antiquity was primarily, on the basis of his writings on Epictetus, that of a φιλόσοφος, it is as an historian that Arrian is mainly known today. More specifically, he is famed as the historian of Alexander: his seven-book *Anabasis Alexandri*, with its single-book accompaniment, the *Indica*, is his only major historical work still extant. This is now generally seen as one of the earliest works in a life-long literary career, which included (aside from the *Anabasis, Indica, Diatribae,* and the shorter essays *Tactics, Cynegeticus* and the *Periplus*) a ten-book account of Trajan's Eastern campaigns known as the *Parthica,* and a major history of his home province, the *Bithyniaca,* described by Arrian in a fragment from the Preface as his fourth historical work, after the biographical essays *Dion* and *Timoleon* and the *Anabasis.*[44]

The picture then emerges of an accomplished scholar and author, whose work was composed concomitantly with a distinguished public and military career – a Greek who moved in the highest circles of the imperial court, and who rose to the summit of the Roman administration. Much has been made of his close association with the philhellene emperor Hadrian, and the two of them embody the complex world of the early second century, in which Greek culture and the old families of the East were raised from the doldrums of the previous two hundred years of Roman occupation.

'Astride two worlds': Arrian and Hadrian

That great flowering of Greek letters and rhetoric looking back to the golden age of hellenic culture is the cultural movement known as the Second Sophistic, best seen in the works of such orators as Dio Chrysostom and Aelius Aristides, as well as those of the biographer and essayist Plutarch (who, like Arrian, wrote a *Dion* and a *Timoleon* in his celebrated *Parallel Lives*). Important elements of this movement were a renewed interest in the classical Greek past, especially in what we would call 'local history', and a corresponding new generation of tourists, who formed the audience for Pausanias' guide to the sights of old Greece.

The most obvious manifestation of this great respect for classical Greek culture in Arrian is clearly visible in his deliberate echoes of the Athenian soldier-philosopher Xenophon. We have already seen that Arrian took his hero's name as part of his own: whether this was a nickname bestowed by his literary *milieu*, or the emperor himself, or even a given name from birth, is unclear,[45] though he does use it to refer to himself in his writings, especially in connection with 'the elder Xenophon' (as he is referred to, for instance, at *Peripl.* 12.5). It was not only a name that they shared: Xenophon, like Arrian, was a soldier as well as an historian, philosopher and essayist; both enjoyed, and wrote treatises on, hunting; both composed instructive memoirs of their youthful studies with great philosophers. Throughout Arrian's *oeuvre* there is a deliberate reflection of his respect for the Athenian, and thus an affinity for the world of classical Greek culture.

But Arrian stands out from the rest of the scholars of the Second Sophistic. Most of the other orators and writers associated with that movement were concerned predominantly with classical Greek culture and literature. Even though Plutarch was clearly familiar with Roman society and religion, and moved in the highest political circles, he never alludes to Virgil or Ovid; and the political orations of

Dio Chrysostom are almost exclusively concerned with petty rivalries for prestige between the cities of his province, Bithynia, or between the aristocrats within them. But in Arrian we see a φιλόσοφος, comfortable in the Greek accent of his cultural *milieu*, spending a career in the imperial administration (possibly even governing a western, Latin-speaking province; see p.4 above), and displaying in his writings concerns peculiar to the Roman *élite* in the immediate imperial circle; the somewhat didactic tone of some of Arrian's Cappadocian works, for example, concerning the activities of a provincial governor, should be compared with the letters of the younger Pliny, which often seem to be lessons in how to be a senator in the new Trajanic era. Rather than simply a product of the Second Sophistic, then, in which Greeks celebrated their own past often without engaging with the external system under which the newly resurgent *poleis* perforce operated, Arrian can be seen as part of a parallel culture, combining elements of the blossoming Greek learning with an awareness of and engagement with Roman society and culture – a culture driven by the person of the Emperor.

It has been noted already that Hadrian was a philhellene – so much so that, as a child in Spain, he was nicknamed *Graeculus*, 'Greekling', and spent so much time on his Greek studies that he had to pay serious attention to his Latin after he had embarked upon his public career.[46] The fact that the peak of the Second Sophistic coincided with his reign and those of his successors Antoninus Pius and Marcus Aurelius has often led to the assumption that Hadrian was responsible for bringing this movement to fruition. The reality is more complex than that.[47] Hadrian was not the first philhellenic emperor – Nero and Domitian could each be described as such – and was not the last; and we have noted that Plutarch (c. AD 46-120) can be seen as one of the forerunners of the Second Sophistic. Yet the emphasis given to this aspect of Hadrian's character in the ancient sources is not accidental, and his championing of the Greek cities of the east was an integral part of his programme as emperor. The *polis* was vital to the Roman administrative structure in the eastern provinces, as is clear from Pliny's correspondence with Trajan, and was in danger of collapsing as the most capable and ambitious young men entered the Roman imperial *cursus* (precisely as Arrian did). Hadrian's numerous benefactions, usually dispensed in person,[48] to the old Greek cities – such as the institution of the Panhellenion at Athens – were calculated to raise their prestige and self-worth:

Now all the Greek cities rise under your leadership, and the monuments dedicated in them and all their embellishments and comforts redound to your honour like beautiful suburbs.[49]

Thus did Hadrian link the flourishing *polis* with the person of the Emperor in the culture of the Empire. While from the earliest days of the principate emperors followed the example of Augustus in placing themselves at the centre of the social and political world of Rome, Hadrian extended this practice in an attempt to forge a common world culture out of the existing Greek and Roman ones: various aspects of his principate – the trend-setting heroic beard, the classical Athenian *erastes-eromenos*, and even Homeric overtones in his relationship with Antinous, and, above all, the extraordinary fusion of Greek and traditional Roman styles employed in his villa at Tivoli[50] – were emphasised to this end. Arrian himself – the soldier-scholar, at home in the Roman and Greek worlds, and friend of the equally ambiguous Emperor – was part of this new order, and his *Periplus Ponti Euxini* affords us a fascinating insight into his world.

3 The *Periplus Ponti Euxini*

The full title of the *Periplus* given at the top of the manuscript is *A Letter of Arrian to Traianus [Hadrianus]: including a Periplus of the Black Sea.* We may consider the two aspects of the opuscule indicated by this label separately: two distinct, but skilfully interwoven, threads running through the work.

The first is the friendly letter. As is only natural for such a form, Arrian's *Periplus* echoes the concerns and interests of its recipient, as Henry Pelham recognised:

Arrian was not only a trusted officer, but the intimate friend of Hadrian, and in the writings of Arrian the character and policy of Hadrian are reflected almost as clearly as the character and policy of Trajan in the letters of the younger Pliny.[51]

The *Periplus* is not the only example of Hadrian's interests influencing the literary output of his circle. We have already (p.4 above) noted the possibly that Arrian was the author of a poem, in Greek, about hunting (another of Hadrian's passions) found in Baetica; and an altar poem in Athens by Vestinus, as Bowie points out, is another instance.[52]

The *Periplus* is, of course, in Greek, which, as we have already noted, was almost Hadrian's first language in his youth, and clearly (as it was for Marcus Aurelius some years later) a natural language of conversation for him. The other preoccupations and themes of Hadrian's principate are all represented.

The principal reason for Arrian's journey in the first place, of course, was to inspect the military installations of the Pontic *limes*. As we might expect, much of the governor's work in this respect was contained in the official Latin report: yet Arrian has no compunction in relating some of the less sensitive information in this open, friendly letter, as if to emphasise Hadrian's genuine interest in the matter.[53] Moving on to the Emperor's private diversions and interests, indicative of the times, we hear much about the various local antiquities of the places visited: for example, the digression on the anchor of the *Argo* (9.2; see note ad loc.). In this connection, too, we have those extraordinarily wide-ranging journeys, unprecedented in their extent. Like that other inveterate traveller, Tennyson's Ulysses and his

> ... grey spirit yearning in desire
> To follow knowledge, like a sinking star,
> Beyond the utmost bound of human thought,

the *Historia Augusta* explained Hadrian's love of travelling as arising from his desire for knowledge:

Peregrinationis ita cupidus ut omnia quae legerat de locis orbis terrarum praesens vellet addiscere.[b]

We can, of course, read certain sections of the *Periplus* as catering for this predilection of Hadrian: Arrian's description of the Isle of Leuke (21-23), with its skilfully attuned references to the story of Achilles and Patroclus that make comparison with Antinous almost irresistible, must surely have whetted his imperial friend's appetite for travel once more. There are also passages that may hint at the previous journeys Hadrian had already made in the region in 123/4 and 129, such as 1.1 and 12.2. Likewise, in the brief aside concerning the village of Athenai (at 5.3), which Fate had him visit when his

---

[b] *SHA Hadrian* 17.8: 'So fond of he was travelling that he wanted to learn further, at first hand, about everything that he had read concerning the different parts of the world'.

fleet took shelter there from a storm, we may almost see the once and future archons of the famous Athens sharing a smile at the memory of the city that meant so much to both of them. But more serious matters take precedence: Arrian justifies his inclusion of the description of the northern and western coasts of the Black Sea by reference not to the various curiosities of that part of the world, but by suggesting the need for information following a potential change in the balance of power in the area (17.3). The *Periplus* can, then, shed as much light upon its recipient as upon its author.

*

So much for the friendly letter, presenting to the reader an image of the emperor by reflecting his concerns. As the second part of the Byzantine title reveals, the other thread of the letter is a *Periplus* – a voyage (more precisely, a circumnavigation), or a written account of one.

The earliest Greek *peripli* we hear of (often reflecting Phoenician and Carthaginian examples) date from the mid-sixth century BC, and seem to have covered areas as far afield as the west African Atlantic coast.[54] Reports of these accounts in later authors suggest to us what sort of information was included in these works. In this period Scylax, admiral of the Persian fleet under Darius I, also wrote an account of his voyage down the Indus river, along the coast of the Arabian peninsula, and up the Red Sea to Arsinoe. The *periplus* that has come down to us under his name, however, is a compilation from the fourth-century BC: yet in this work there are dim signs of the development of a literary genre from dry lists of places and distances, with asides on local produce and the like.[55] Slightly later than this compilation came the *periplus* of Nearchus the Cretan, who scouted out the coast of the Indian Ocean on the orders of Alexander. Substantial fragments are preserved in Arrian's *Indica*, the companion book to the *Anabasis*, and these include notes on zoological and geographical phenomena, as well as the military information that was the primary focus of the work.

This work of Nearchus, obviously familiar to Arrian, must have influenced the choice of form for the *Periplus*; Arrian's original mission, after all, like Nearchus', was a voyage of military inspection. Nor did the military tradition of geographical scholarship end with Alexander: it was his conquests that marked a watershed in the important link between military expeditions and geographical exploration. He was the first to combine conquest with discovery on a global scale, employing not only men like Nearchus at sea, but also a group known as *bematistai*, who measured the roads trodden by the King's army as it advanced through unknown territory, keeping and publishing notes on geographical features and place names.[56] When a later generation of world-conquerors rose towards the end of the Roman Republic, accounts of their expeditions too became vital repositories of geographical knowledge for later scholars and emperors alike.[57] But geography also became a vital

tool of their imagery. Pompey took with him the
Greek historian Theophanes of Mytilene on his
eastern campaigns, and Caesar's *commentarii* on his
wars in Gaul and Germany – previously on the
bounds of Roman geographical knowledge – were
perhaps more about portraying the author as a world
conqueror than they were about politics or military
affairs.

Augustus was particularly adept at playing this
game. The expeditions of Aelius Gallus to Arabia
Felix and C. Petronius to the southern Egyptian
deserts in the early part of his reign – and the official
records of them reflected in the accounts of Strabo
and the elder Pliny – were all concerned purely with
the pursuit of *gloria* in the subjugation of vast
swathes of evocative geography, and the mighty
rivers Rhine, Danube and Euphrates that marked
the bounds of Roman rule by Augustus' death were
chosen as much for their almost mythological
resonance as for their strategic value.[58] This theme
continues in the great public works carried out by
the Flavians, celebrated as demonstrating the
Roman mastery of the natural world.[59]

Arrian's work is a direct descendant of these earlier
accounts of military exploration. It is clear that such
works were still intended to serve something like
their original purpose: our author leaves a trace of
this in his direct link of exploration to impending
military action in the notice of the death of Kotys
(17.3). But it is an example not only of the
contribution to geographical knowledge made by
Roman commanders, but also of the evocation of

geographical features and landmarks to illustrate the scope of Roman rule. It is in this context that Arrian's comment at 15.1 – that the river Halys, which, in Classical times, separated the great kingdoms of Lydia and Persia, 'now flows under Roman rule' – can be understood. Once again, the expression of this tradition in a *periplus* was a deliberate harnessing by Arrian of an historical Greek form for purposes the Romans had made their own.

But this form of geographical monograph was of course also particularly well-suited to describe the Black Sea, whose entire coastline could be – and had been – treated in this unified way.[60] Arrian therefore had precedent enough for casting his work in this form. The model of the *periplus* provided a framework which would easily accommodate the narrative of a voyage of inspection – the pretext for writing the letter to Hadrian in the first place – as well as plenty of scope, given the development of the genre, for the inclusion of material of more general interest to the reader. Thus Arrian – again demonstrating the ease with which he could work in an idiom deriving elements from both Greece and Rome – could incorporate his letter, concerned as it was with contemporary issues facing the Roman empire and its *princeps*, within a form that was both a successor to a long-established tradition of Greek scholarship and a suggestion of the power of military exploration in the sophisticated imagery of the Roman emperors.

So, the *Periplus* is at once both revealing private correspondence and a new take on the traditional Greek scholarly geographical treatise, mixed with the Roman military report: a work fully representative of the times, and of the author those times produced.

Structure and authenticity

One of the first things that one notices upon reading the *Periplus* (especially considering other examples of the literary *genre* to which its title would suggest it belongs) is that its structure and composition are rather odd. This has, since the later nineteenth century, sometimes led its status as a genuine member of Arrian's *corpus* to be doubted, first by Brandis in 1896 and later by Kiessling, Minns and Chapot.[61] We have already noted the dual character of the work: this goes some way towards explaining the oddity, as will become apparent, but more needs to be said on this tricky question.

A brief summary of the structure of the work may be useful. Ostensibly a letter from Arrian to Hadrian, the first part of the work (up to chapter 11) describes Arrian's official tour of inspection of the features and military installations of the Cappadocian coastline, from the headquarters of the Pontic Fleet at Trapezous to Sebastopolis, the last Roman town on the east coast of the Black Sea. At chapter 12, there is an abrupt break where begins a passage (which runs to the end of 17.1) in the form of a 'flashback', describing the coastline from

Byzantium as far as Trapezous. Chapters 18 to 25, the end of the work, resume the description of the coast from Dioskourias and follow it round, anticlockwise, to Byzantium, thus completing the description of the Black Sea coasts. This time, though, there is a bridge paragraph (17.2-3), summing up the journey from Byzantium to Dioskourias, and supplying the reason for continuing the description – namely, that, following the death of the ruler of the Bosporan kingdom, the Emperor would need information concerning the region upon which to decide Roman policy. The description thus continues without a break, all the way round to Byzantium, completing the *Periplus*.

It is beyond question that a *Periplus Ponti Euxini* attributed to Arrian was known in late antiquity: it is mentioned explicitly by the fifth- or sixth-century lexicographer Stephanus of Byzantium as an authority for several of his entries. Further, the sixth-century historian Procopius directly attacks some of its premises in his geographical excursus on the Black Sea, although not citing the work by name.[62] Neither the work of Stephanus, however, nor that of Procopius, can be used to guarantee the authenticity of the *Periplus* as we have it. The lexicographer's only explicit reference to that work is confined to material presented in the first eleven chapters of the *Periplus* that we have;[63] and Pekkanen has shown that the work Procopius referred to need not have been anything other than the same eleven chapters, since parallels with later passages of Arrian may very plausibly have been derived from other sources.[64] In any case, in one passage Procopius laments the fact that he cannot give exact distances for the whole circuit of the Black Sea, as earlier writers had similarly been unable,[65] and so demonstrably cannot have had Arrian's *Periplus Ponti Euxini*, as we know it, in front of him. Pekkanen, however, does allow the possibility that Procopius' material was only indirectly derived from Arrian, or that the later author used the same source as Arrian for the part of his work in which he appears to be attacking Arrian's own conclusions.[66]

Chapot, summing up the debate as it stood in 1921, rejected Arrian's authorship of the *Periplus* we have, and postulated that it is a pre-Byzantine compilation – possibly from as early as the end of the second century[67] – incorporating a genuine letter from Arrian to Hadrian, being chapters 1-11 of the work as we have it. The principal argument was that the unorthodox – even unique – structure pointed to a maladroit forger. That this is possible is demonstrated by the existence of a Byzantine work now known as the 'Anonymous *Periplus Ponti Euxini*', owing to our ignorance of its author – or rather, its compiler.[68] For this work is in fact portions of several other descriptions of the Black Sea – the *Peripli* of Menippus and Arrian, and the verse *Perigesis* addressed to King Nicomedes of Bithynia, with a few small extracts from Pseudo-Scylax – collected under Arrian's name, and reproducing the salutation found at the top of Arrian's letter, in an attempt (as Diller thinks) to enhance the value of the work from the attribution.

But the fact that the compiler of this piece managed to incorporate the salutation and outward form of Arrian's letter, while interpolating later portions of Arrian and others in order to describe the coast continuously from Byzantium in an anti-clockwise direction (i.e. to make the structure of Arrian's work conform to a conventional *Periplus* form) indicate that one forger, at any rate, did not feel constrained to put the entire 'letter' (chapters 1-11) of Arrian first, simply because he wished to use its basic form.

Defenders of the *Periplus*' authenticity have further argued that the ambitious structure is justifiable, even admirable, and, further, that the detail and complexity of the whole work is beyond the average forger.[69] Silberman, with justice, posed the question of why such an odd structure should be *prima facie* evidence of forgery:

Mais on se demande bien pourquoi un faussaire aurait volontairement adopté un plan en effet aussi bizarre, qui n'eût pas manqué d'éveiller les soupçons. Quant à voir dans ce plan, comme on l'a fait, la ruse au second degré d'un plaigaire commettant volontairement une maladresse 'pour faire plus vrai', cela paraît tout à fait invraisemblable, et témoignerait de scrupules étrangers aux auteurs antiques.[c]

---

[c] Silberman (1978), p.158: 'But one must ask oneself why a forger would willingly adopt such a strange plan, which would not fail to arouse suspicion. As for seeing this plan, as it has been, as a plagiariser's double-bluff, deliberately committing a solecism "to make it seem more genuine", this would appear utterly unlikely, and would attest to scruples alien to ancient authors.'

He, and others, in any case saw the structure as eminently explicable. Firstly, to create a proper *Periplus*, one must perforce travel either left or right from a starting point at the Bosporus.[70] To accept Patsch's ingenious solution of transposing the second and third sections of the work as we have it would be to create a *Periplus* starting and finishing at Trapezous, which is too radical a departure from the traditional form that binds the work.[71] Secondly, it must be remembered that the structure is not the principal feature of importance. The work is a letter, first and foremost, and it is only natural that the primary subject of the letter – that is, the inspection – should be related first. The *Periplus* form is used (albeit in the background in the first section, and increasingly prominently later on) as a vehicle for a literary composition, almost as an excuse for Arrian to continue his description beyond his initial brief, and so to divert Hadrian's (and the public's) imagination with set-piece descriptions of the island of Leuke, for instance, or of the landscape, heavy with history, where Xenophon and the Ten Thousand once trod.

Bosworth, in this vein, viewed the structure of the *Periplus*, not as *maladresse*, but as evidence of a literary craftsman at the height of his powers, 'a very sensitive and allusive piece by a mature and experienced writer'.[72] Furthermore, the style of the *Periplus* – in particular, the Xenophontic aspects of the work discussed above – was perfectly consistent with the style of Arrian as witnessed in his other extant works. Silberman has even noted several

examples of a consistency of style across the work
(despite the apparent unevenness at first glance),
one of which is the equivalence of the two traditional
landmark rivers Phasis and Ister in the literary
schemes of the descriptions of the west and east
shores.[73] But it is a comparison of the literary style
of the second and third sections of the *Periplus* with
Arrian's other works that is most instructive, with
many episodes for instance structured to begin with
an exposition of fact, with a formula of report (such
as οἱ δὲ καὶ τάδε ἱστοροῦσιν, 'they also report these
things, that...', at *Peripl.* 22.1) then introducing a
more florid passage, as in the *Anabasis*,[74] or the
mixture of personal observations and literary
references so characteristic of all Arrian's work.

A further characteristically Arrianic feature of the
Periplus, particularly marked in the first few
chapters and in the second section of the work, is the
frequent allusion to Xenophon – the classical author,
as mentioned above, to whom Arrian looked for much
of his inspiration, and whose visit to the southern
shore of the Black Sea with the Ten Thousand is
echoed so strongly in Arrian's treatment of that part
of his work.

It would be a brilliant forger indeed who could not
only imitate so precisely and plausibly the style of
his chosen target, and come up with a such a bold
structure to deal with that target's supposed
circumstances, but who could also incorporate such
details as the implicit reference to Hadrian and
Antinous at 23.4, so pertinent in 132, only two years
after the young man's death, but which surely faded

from the public consciousness when the fresh foibles of new emperors emerged: a forger so brilliant, indeed, that all his other efforts have gone undetected, presumably among the accepted works of other authors – for no other antique forgery so far recognised is as inventive and learned as this one would be.

Silberman, in his 1993 article, declared the controversy closed, in favour of authenticity, and, despite the nagging concerns that may remain, the consensus now seems to be that we are as sure as we can be, given the extremely limited transmission of the work, that the *Periplus Ponti Euxini* is a genuine work of Arrian's. It is to this transmission that we now turn.

Transmission

We are fortunate that Arrian's *Periplus* has survived at all. Like the works of Catullus, or nine of Euripides' plays, it has come down to us through the 'dark age' of classical Greek literature in only one manuscript, in this case the *codex Palatinus Heidelbergensis graecus* 398,[75] dating from the ninth century, and referred to as 'P'. This source, then, must provide the basis for any text – although the Anonymous *Periplus* (the latter portion of which is also preserved in this manuscript, designated 'p') is useful in that it provides an (albeit limited) parallel tradition for the incorporated material taken from Arrian. The Anonymous *Periplus* is also transmitted (in its entirety) in the *codex Londiniensis add.* 19391, or 'I', part of a larger manuscript copied from the *Palatinus*, and (the beginning only) in the *codex Vaticanus graecus* 143, known as 'v'.

The standard modern edition is that of Roos in the Teubner *scripta minora* of Arrian, revised in 1967 by Wirth, replacing Hercher's 1885 revision of the 1854 Teubner edition of Eberhard. Also of value are the editions of 1958, with an Italian translation, by Marenghi, and of 1995, with a French translation, by Silberman. The most recently published English translation was that of Thomas Falconer in 1805. The present edition follows the now standard division into chapters established by the 1846 edition of Müller and taken up by most subsequent editors; it should be noted, however, that the division later used by Müller in his 1855 edition of the *Geographi Graeci Minores* is different.

A particular problem in establishing a text from a single manuscript is highlighted in the *Periplus* of Arrian: that is, how to decide between alternative spellings or dialect renditions of the same word (as between the manuscript readings of θάλαττα and θάλασσα in the very first paragraph). Arrian was perfectly capable of writing in different dialects according to the style of the work – the *Cynegeticus* imitates Xenophon's Attic, whereas the *Indica* uses the Ionic of Herodotus – but it is difficult to decide which (if either) was the author's original intention in an opuscule directly attested by only one manuscript. Müller, Roos, Marenghi, and (more recently) Silberman have all taken the approach that, given the paucity of the tradition, it is preferable simply to reproduce the manuscript reading, keeping all discrepancies. It seems to me, though, given the strong Xenophontic influence upon the *Periplus*, that Attic dialect variants can safely be given preference, and this edition therefore 'corrects' (except, of course, in quotations) all non-Attic spellings of words attested in Attic forms elsewhere in the text.[76]

4 Conclusion

In the final analysis, then, why should Arrian's *Periplus* warrant attention at all, let alone a new edition and translation? To be sure, it is not the author's most stylish work, despite its undoubted erudition and literary skill; for all its structural inventiveness, the form often seems laboured rather than audacious. But as an historical document, it is unique. Written by a man at the pinnacle of his career, it gives us a vital glimpse of the dynamics of a remarkable, yet obscure, part of the Roman world, and some idea of how such a place could be governed and controlled within the flexibility of the Roman system. Written by a man standing astride two worlds, and addressed to the master of both, it offers us an insight into the workings of the elusive Hadrian through his friend and servant who, though born at the opposite end of the Roman dominions, shared (or at least understood) the convictions and aims of his Emperor. Written by a man who grew up in the traditions of the classical Greek authors, it demonstrates how a conventional, scholarly form could be adapted by a literary craftsman to incorporate interesting local legend, useful strategic information, and subtle encomium of Rome's *Princeps*. Above all, written by a man who was perhaps the most representative of the culture of his age, it affords us an epitome of that culture in a tightly packed nutshell. It is a nutshell well worth opening.

Notes

1 Plato, *Phaedo* 109b.
2 The principal discussions are to be found in Syme (1982) and Stadter (1980) ch.1, superseding the long-standard article of E. Schwartz in *RE* II.1 (1896) 1230-47.
3 The *praenomen* is confirmed by an inscription from Athens, *AE* 1971.437.
4 Thus Syme (1982), pp.187-8, although Stadter (1980), p.6, suggests a senatorial background for the family on account of its early admission to the citizenship.
5 F.G.B. Millar ('Epictetus and the imperial court', *JRS* 55 [1965] 141-8) assigns a date of 108; internal evidence of Arrian's *Diatribae* indicates that his studies started no earlier than 105, the end of the Dacian wars.
6 *Scriptores Historiae Augustae, Vita Hadriani* 16.10.
7 Arrian, *Indica* 4.15-16; see Bosworth (1993), p.229.
8 Stadter (1980), p.9.
9 *AE* 1974.370.
10 Arrian, *Anabasis* II.16.4.
11 *CIL* XV.244, 532 for the brick stamps.
12 Syme (1982), p.200. Arrian is known to have been in place as governor of Cappadocia by 131; see the allusion at *Peripl.* 17.3 to the recent death of King Kotys II of the Bosporan Kingdom – an event known to have taken place in the year 131/2.
13 See A.B. Bosworth, 'Vespasian's reorganisation of the north-east frontier', *Antichthon* 10 (1976) 63-78.
14 See notes to 1.1 and 16.6 for more on Trapezous as a military port.

15 Tacitus, *Annales* XIII.39; see also Rostovtzeff (1957), p.141.
16 Thus Reddé (1986), pp.441-3.
17 Strabo XI.496; see Braund (1989), pp.31-9.
18 For the cultural and historical background of ancient Colchis, see Lordkipanidze (1983), pp.123-42. A fuller discussion of the Argonautic connections can be found in the Commentary, ad loc.
19 Colchis may have had the earliest mint for silver coins in the Black Sea: see Boardman (1962/3) pp.50-1.
20 See Strabo XII.3.1-2 for a brief history of pre-Roman Pontus and Colchis.
21 Tacitus, *Historiae* I.6; Pliny, *Natural History* VI.15; cf. Strabo XI.2.16.
22 Tacitus, *Hist.* III.47-8.
23 See Hippocrates, *Airs, Waters and Places* 15 for a description of the country in antiquity.
24 Braund (1989), p.38.
25 See also Tacitus, *Ann.* XVI.23, 'Tiridates accipiendo Armeniae regno adventabat'.
26 *ILS* 8795.   Further, *AE* 1951.263 is the dedication of a centurion of XII Fulminata on the Caspian coast of Albania.
27 *SHA, Hadr.* 13.9
28 To the extent that Pharasmenes even visited Rome as Hadrian's guest: *SHA, Hadr.* 9.3; Dio Cassius LXIX.25.2. See Syme (1981) for a full discussion of the divergent traditions.
29 For the suggestion that Pharasmenes was encroaching on Colchis, see Syme (1981), p.280.
30 The Latin report that accompanied the *Periplus* is referred to twice, at 6.2 and 10.1.
31 See also Speidel (1986); Braund (1991) for the fort at Apsaros.
32 See Arrian, *Ectaxis*.
33 Speidel (1986), p.658.
34 See n.22 above (Anicetus); Zosimus I.32-3 (Scythians).
35 *ILS* 8801 (Hadrian's anniversary); *ILS* 1066 (Arrian's successor, Burbuleius).
36 See Syme (1982), pp.203-4, 205-6.
37 *IG* II2 2055; Stadter (1980), pp.16-17.
38 For such a suggestion, see Schwartz (1896), p.1231; refuted by Bosworth (1993), p.232, and Syme (1982), pp.207-9.
39 Stadter (1980), p.18, with nn.104 and 105 (Herodes and Rusticus); p.14 with n.89 (statue).
40 E.g. Photius 17b 15-17.
41 Arrian, *Cyn.* 1.4; *Anab.* I.12.5.
42 For a full statement of both positions, and a refutation of Schwartz, see Bosworth (1972).

43 Pliny, *Epistulae* I.10; cf. III.5.

44 Arrian, *Bithyniaca* fr.1.3.

45 Stadter (1980), pp.2-3, suggests that it could be an integral part of his given name, a Greek name to be used alongside his Roman *nomen*, as in the case of Plutarch (whose *nomen* was Mestrius).

46 *SHA, Hadr.* 1.5 (*Graeculus*); 3.1 (rusty Latin).

47 See M.T. Boatwright, *Hadrian and the Cities of the Roman Empire* (Princeton, 2000).

48 See H.W. Benario, *A Commentary on the* Vita Hadriani *in the* Historia Augusta (1980), appendix 4, for a valuable synopsis of the Emperor's travels.

49 Aelius Aristides, *Ad Romam* 94.

50 See W.L. MacDonald and J.A. Pinto, *Hadrian's Villa and its Legacy* (New Haven, 1995): "In Hadrian's day, Greek culture regained lost momentum and Greek art took a leading place within the Roman frame. Of all this Hadrian's Villa is an elaborate portrait, as it is also of the man most fully representative of the age" (p.23).

51 Pelham (1896), p.626.

52 See Bowie (2002), p.191.

53 E.g. the reference to the strength of the garrison at Phasis, 9.3-5.

54 See Dilke (1985), ch.9 'Periploi'.

55 Ibid., p.134.

56 See Pliny, *NH* VI.61; Sherk (1974).

57 See Sherk (1974); Millar (1982), esp. pp.15-19.

58 The common notion that Augustus' foreign policy was essentially defensive, influenced possibly more by the Hadrianic concerns of Tacitus' narrative than the Augustan reality, should now be viewed with a healthy scepticism. See Appian, *Praefatio* 4/14-15 for an example of the fluid nature of the conception of these rivers as geographical signposts rather than as 'frontiers'.

59 For a Flavian celebration in this mould of the completion of the *via Domitiana* (AD 95), see Statius, *Silvae* IV.3: see also Dio Cassius for Trajan's bridge (cf. Caesar's bridge over the Rhine, *De Bello Gallico* IV.17).

60 See Baschmakoff (1948) for an overview of all the known examples of this sub-genre.

61 Brandis (1896); Kiessling (1913); Minns (1913); Chapot (1921).

62 Procopius, *De Bellis Justiniani* VIII.1-6 (geography of the Black Sea); the passages accepted as parallel to Arrian are VIII.2.10 (cf. *Peripl.* 4.1), VIII.2.11 (cf. *Peripl.* 6.2-3), and

38   *Arrian: Periplus Ponti Euxini*

VIII.1.8-10 (cf. *Peripl.* 11.1). Arrian is mentioned by name by Procopius only at VIII.14.48, although it is in connection with a passage not extant in the works of Arrian.

63 This is the entry on the tribe called the Ἀψίλαι: 'ἔθνος Σκυθικόν, γειτνίαζον Λάζους, ὡς Ἀρριανὸς ἐν Περίπλῳ τοῦ Εὐξείνου Πόντου'; cf. *Peripl.* 11.3. Three other names in the first eleven chapters, and two in chapters 12-16, are also cited ὡς Ἀρριανός, without specifying a work. One of these, Ἀλμήνη, does not feature in the *Periplus*; although Müller, in his 1855 edition of *Peripl.*, has suggested that this is a corruption of Ἀρμένη, found at *Peripl.* 14.4.

64 Pekkanen (1964).

65 Procopius, *De Bellis* VIII.5.32.

66 Pekkanen (1964), pp.43, 51.

67 Chapot (1921), pp.152, 154.

68 The best edition, with notes and an introduction, is Diller (1952), ch.4   He argues for a later sixth-century date, though allowing that it may be later (pp.109-13).   It was certainly known by the late tenth-/early eleventh-century historian Leo Diaconus, who cites a passage 'in Arrian's *Periplus*' (IX.6, p.150 in the Bonn edition, Ἀρριανὸς γάρ φησιν ἐν τῷ Περίπλῳ ...') which is not in that work as we have it, and turns out to belong to the Anonymous *Periplus*.

69 Defences of the *Periplus*' authenticity, more or less rigorous, include: Reuss (1901); Patsch (1904); Rostovtzeff (1931); Roos (1926); Baschmakoff (1948); Marenghi (1958); Bosworth (1993); and Silberman (1978, 1993 and 1995).

70 Baschmakoff (1948) compares the structure of the known *peripli Ponti Euxini*, noting that the Roman-era works tend to travel ἐν δεξιᾷ from the Bosporus, i.e. anticlockwise, in contrast to the earlier works of Hecataeus, Ps.-Scylax, and Ephorus, who traced their route in the opposite direction.

71 Patsch (1904).

72 Bosworth (1993), p.250.

73 Silberman (1978), pp.161-2.

74 Cf. the example cited with *Anab.* IV.14.2; V.2.7; VII.1.2, 26.3; *Ind.* 8.8.

75 This manuscript also contains the only source of Arrian's *Cynegeticus*.

76 See the Note on the Text for a full list of these changes.

Bibliography

Anderson, J.G.C. (1971), 'The eastern frontier from Tiberius to Nero' in *Cambridge Ancient History* vol.10, pp.743-80

Bashmakov, A.A. (1948), *La synthèse des périples pontiques, méthode de précision en paléo-ethnographie* (Paris)

Boardman, J. (1962/3), 'Greek Archaeology on the shores of the Black Sea', *Journal of Hellenic Studies Archaeological Reports 1962-63*, pp.34-51

----- (1980), *The Greeks Overseas* (3rd ed., London)

Bosworth, A.B. (1972), 'Arrian's literary development', *Classical Quarterly* 22, pp.163-85

----- (1977), 'Arrian and the Alani', *Harvard Studies in Classical Philology* 81, pp.217-55

----- (1993), 'Arrian and Rome: the minor works' in *Aufstieg und Niedergang der Römischen Welt* II.34.1, pp.226-75

Bounegru, O. and Zahariade, M. (1996), *Les forces navales du Bas Danube et de la Mer Noire aux Ier-Vième siècles* (Oxford)

Bowie, E. (2002), 'Hadrian and Greek Poetry' in Ostenfeld, E.N., ed., *Greek Romans and Roman Greeks: studies in cultural interaction* (Aarhus Studies in Mediterranean Antiquity III; Aarhus)

Brandis, C.G. (1896), 'Arrians Periplus Ponti Euxini', *Rheinisches Museum* 51, pp.109-26

Braund, D.C. (1989), 'Coping with the Caucasus: Roman responses to local conditions in Colchis' in French & Lightfoot (q.v.)

----- (1991), 'Hadrian and Pharasmenes', *Klio* 73, pp.208-19

----- (1994), *Georgia in Antiquity: a history of Colchis and transcaucasian Iberia 550 BC-AD 562* (Oxford)

Bryer, A.A.M. and Winfield, D.C. (1985), *The Byzantine Monuments and Topography of the Pontus* (Dumbarton Oaks Studies 20; Washington)

Burney, C. and Lang, D.M. (1971), *The Peoples of the Hills: ancient Ararat and Caucasus* (London)

Chapot, V. (1921), 'Arrien et le Périple du Pont-Euxin', *Revue des Etudes Grecques* 34, pp.129-54

Chevallier, R. (1988), *Voyages et déplacements dans l'Empire romain* (Paris)

Chotard, H. (1960), *Le Périple de la Mer Noire par Arrien* (Paris)

Diller, A. (1952), *The Tradition of the Minor Greek Geographers* (New York)

Dilke, O.A.W. (1985), *Greek and Roman Maps* (London)

Drews, R. (1976), 'The earliest Greek settlements on the Black Sea', *Journal of Hellenic Studies* 96, pp.18-31

Eberhard, A. and Hercher, R. (1885), *Arriani Nicomediensis Scriptora Minora* (Leipzig)

French, D. and Lightfoot, C. (1989) eds, *The Eastern Frontier of the Roman Empire: Proceedings of a colloquium held at Ankara in September 1988* (British Institute of Archaeology at Ankara, Monograph 11) (Oxford)

Fossey, J.M. (1997), ed., *Proceedings of the First International Conference on the Archaeology and History of the Black Sea* (Amsterdam)

Gamkrelidze, G. (1992), 'Hydroarchaeology in the Georgian Republic (the Colchian Littoral)', *International Journal of Nautical Archaeology* 21, pp.101-9

Gigauri, C.V. (1988), *La Colchide dans la littérature romaine* (Tblisi)

Gorbunova, K.S. (1971/2), 'Archaeological investigations on the northern shore of the Black Sea in the territory of the Soviet Union, 1965-70', *Journal of Hellenic Studies Archaeological Reports 1971-72*, pp.48-59

Hamilton, W.J. (1842), *Researches in Asia Minor, Pontus and Armenia* (London)

Henderson, B.W. (1923), *The Life and Principate of the Emperor Hadrian* (London)

Hind, J.G.F. (1983/4), 'Greek and barbarian peoples on the shores of the Black Sea', *Journal of Hellenic Studies Archaeological Reports 1983-84*, pp.71-97

----- (1992/3), 'Archaeology of the Greeks and barbarian peoples around the Black Sea 1982-92', *Journal of Hellenic Studies Archaeological Reports 1992-93*, pp.82-112

Hodinnott, R.F. (1975), *Bulgaria in Antiquity: an archaeological introduction* (London)

Jones, A.H.M. (1971), *The Cities of the Eastern Roman Provinces* (2nd ed., Oxford)

Kacharava, D.D. (1983/4), 'Archaeological investigations on the eastern Black Sea littoral, 1970-1980', *Journal of Hellenic Studies Archaeological Reports 1983-84*, pp.98-101

----- (1991/2), 'Archaeology in Georgia 1980-1990', *Journal of Hellenic Studies Archaeological Reports 1991-92*, pp.79-86

Khartchilava, T. and Geny, E. (1990), eds, *Le Pont-Euxin vu par les Grecs* (Paris)

Kiessling, M. (1913), 'Ἡνίοχοι' in Pauly-Wissowa, *Real-Encyclopädie*, vol. 8

Koromela, M. (1991), *The Greeks in the Black Sea: from the Bronze Age to the early twentieth century* (Athens)

Lévêque, P. (1992), 'Recherches nouvelles sur le Pont-Euxin', *Revue des Etudes Anciennes* 94, pp.49-56

Levkinadze, V.A. (1969), 'The Pontic *limes*', *Vestnik Drevnei Istorii* 108, pp.75-93

Lomouri, N.Y. (1957), 'Iz istoricheskoy geografii drevnei Kolkhidy', *Vestnik Drevnei Istorii* 4, pp.96-110

Lordkipanidze, O. (1974), 'La Géorgie et le monde grec', *Bulletin de Correspondence Hellénique* 98, pp.897-948

----- (1983), 'The Greco-Roman world and ancient Georgia (Colchis and Iberia)', in *Modes de contacts et processus de transformation dans les sociétés antiques: actes du colloque de Cortone (24-30 mai 1981)* (Pisa and Rome), pp.123-4

Marenghi, G. (1957), 'Carattere e intenti del Periplo di Arriano', *Athenaeum* NS 35 III-IV, pp.117-92

----- (1958), ed., *Arriano: Periplo del Ponti Eusini* (Naples)

Minns, E.H. (1913), *Scythians and Greeks: a survey of ancient history and archaeology on the north coast of the Euxine from the Danube to the Caucasus* (Cambridge)

Mitford, T.B. (1974), 'Some inscriptions from the Cappadocian *limes*', *Journal of Roman Studies* 64, pp.160-75

----- (1980), 'Cappadocia and Armenia Minor: historical setting of the *limes*', in *Aufstieg und Niedergang der Römischen Welt* II.7.2, pp.1169-228

Müller, C.F.W. (1855), *Geographi Graeci Minores* (Paris)

Nawotka, K. (1989), 'The attitude towards Rome in the political propaganda of the Bosporan monarchs', *Latomus* 48, pp.326-38

Nicolet, C. (1988), *L'Inventaire du Monde: géographie et politique aux origines de l'Empire romain* (Paris)

Patsch, C.L. (1904), 'Arrians Periplus Ponti Euxini', *Klio* 4, pp.68-75

Pekkanen, T. (1964), 'Procopius and the *Periplus* of Arrian', *Eranos* 62, pp.40-51

Pelham, H. (1896), 'Arrian as Legate of Cappadocia', *English Historical Review* 11, pp.625-40

Reddé, M. (1986), *Mare Nostrum: les infrastructures, le dispositif et l'histoire de la marine militaire sous l'Empire romain* (Rome)

Reuss, F. (1901), 'Zu Arrians Περίπλους Πόντου Εὐξείνου', *Rheinisches Museum* 56, pp.367-91

Rice, T.T. (1961), *The Scythians* (London)

Roos, A.G. (1926), 'Ad Ursulum Philippum Boissevain septuagenarium epistula de Arriani Periplo Ponti Euxini', *Mnemosyne* 54, pp.101-17

----- and Wirth, G. (1967), *Flavii Arriani quae existant omnia* (Leipzig)

Rostovtzeff, M. (1957), *Social and Economic History of the Roman Empire* (2ⁿᵈ ed., Oxford)

Shelov, D.B. (1980), 'Colchis in the Pontic Empire of Mithridates VI', *Vestnik Drevnei Istorii* 153, pp.28-43

----- (1981), 'The Romans in the north Black Sea area, 2ⁿᵈ century AD', *Vestnik Drevnei Istorii* 158, pp.52-63

Sherk, R. (1974), 'Roman geographical exploration and military maps', *Aufstieg und Niedergang der Römischen Welt* II.1, pp.534-62

Silberman, A. (1978), 'Quelques remarques sur la composition du Périple d'Arrien', *Revue des Etudes Grecques* 91, pp.158-64

----- (1993), 'Arrien, *Périple du Pont-Euxin*: Essai d'interprétation et d'évaluation des données géographiques et historiques', in *Aufstieg und Niedergang der Römischen Welt* II.34.1, pp.276-311

----- (1995), ed., *Arrien: Périple du Pont-Euxin* (Paris)

Speidel, M.P. (1986), 'The Caucasus frontier: second century garrison at Apsarus, Petra and Phasis' in *Studien zu den Militärgrenzen Roms III* (Stuttgart), pp.657-60

Stadter, P.A. (1980), *Arrian of Nicomedia* (Chapel Hill)

Starr, C.G. (1960), *Roman Imperial Navy, 31 BC-334 AD* (Cambridge)

Syme, R. (1981), 'Hadrian and the Vassal Princes', *Athenaeum* 59, pp.276f.

----- (1982), 'The career of Arrian', *Harvard Studies in Classical Philology* 86, pp.171-211

Talbert, R.J.A. (2000), ed., *The Barrington Atlas of Ancient History* (Princeton)

Tonnet, H. (1988), *Recherches sur Arrien: sa personnalité et ses écrits atticistes* (Amsterdam)

Trejster, M.J. and Vinogradov, Y.G. (1993), 'Archaeology on the northern coast of the Black Sea', *American Journal of Archaeology* 97, pp.521-63

Tsetskhladze, G.R. (1994), ed., *Greek and Roman Settlements on the Black Sea Coast* (Bradford)

----- (1996), *New Studies on the Black Sea Littoral* (Oxford)

Vidal-Naquet, P. (1984), 'Flavius Arrianus entre deux mondes', an introductory essay to Savinel, P., *L'Histoire d'Alexandre d'Arrien* (Paris)

Wheeler, E.L. (1977), *Flavius Arrianus: a political and military biography* (Duke University)

Note on the Text

The text employed in this edition is based on that of Roos and Wirth in the 1967 Teubner edition; changes from that edition (excluding minor ones of punctuation, etc.) are noted below.

1.1 θάλατταν for θάλασσαν
1.3 ἀποδείκνυσι for ἀποδείκνυσιν
2.1 φαύλως for φαῦλος (following Hercher, cf. l)
3.4 ἐπεισέρρει for ἐπεισρέει (following P)
4.1 ἔστι for ἔστιν
4.2 ἀλλ᾽ οὐ for ἀλλὰ οὐ
4.3 ἀλλ᾽ εἰς for ἀλλὰ εἰς
4.4 θάλατταν for θάλασσαν
6.3 τοὔνομα for τὸ ὄνομα
7.1 εἰς for ἐς
7.3 τετταράκοντα for τεσσαράκοντα
7.4 εἰς Ἄρχαβιν for ἐς Ἄ.; εἰς πεντεκαίδεκα for ἐς π.
7.5 ἀπ᾽ Ἀκινάσου for ἀπὸ Ἀκ.
8.1 χρόαν for χροιὰν (following Hercher)
8.2 πρὸ for πρὸς (following MSS); θαλάττῃ for θαλάσσῃ
8.3 θάλαττα for θάλασσα
8.4 θαλάττῃ for θαλάσσῃ; θάλαττην for θάλασσην
8.5 Roos adds 'εἰσπλέοντας' following 'εἰς αὐτόν'; εἰσβαίνωσιν for εἰσβάλλωσιν (following P)
9.4 ἐν ὀλίγῳ for ἑνὶ λόγῳ (following P)
9.5 στρατιᾶς for στρατείας (following P)
10.1 εἰς for ἐς
10.2 εἰς for ἐς

10.3 ἀπ᾽ Ἀστελέφου for ἀπὸ Ἀστ.

11.2 Roos gives Ζυδρειτῶν δ᾽ ἐχόμενοι Λαζοί from l

11.3 δ᾽ αὐτῶν for δὲ αὐτῶν

11.5 ὑφ᾽ Ἡφαίστου for ὑπὸ Ἡφαίστου

12.2 ἐστι στενότατον for ἐστιν στ.

12.3 εἰς for ἐς

12.5 ἐστὶ for ἐστὶν; θαλάττῃ for θαλάσσῃ

13.1 εἰσβάλλει for ἐσβάλλει

13.2 εἰς Κάλητα for ἐς Κ.

13.3 εἰς Λύκον for ἐς Λ.

13.4 τετταράκοντα for τεσσαράκοντα, twice; ἀπ᾽ Ὀξίνου for ἀπὸ Ὀξ.

14.1 εἰς Ἄμαστριν for ἐς Ἄμ.; ἀπ᾽ Ἐρυθίνων for ἀπὸ Ἐρ.

14.2 εἰς δὲ Θύμηνα for ἐς δὲ Θ.

14.3 εἰς Αἰγινήτην for ἐς Αἰγ.

14.4 εἰς Στεφάνην for ἐς Στ.; εἰς Ἀρμένην for ἐς Ἀρ.

15.1 ἀλλ᾽ ἀπὸ for ἀλλὰ ἀπὸ

15.2 Κωνωπεῖον and Κωνωπείου for Κωνώπιον and Κωνωπίου (following P); εἰς for ἐς, three times

15.3 εἰς Ἡράκλειον for ἐς Ἡρ.; τετταράκοντα for τεσσαράκοντα

16.1 εἰς Οἰνόην for ἐς Οἰ.; εἰς Φιγαμοῦντα for ἐς Φιγ.; ἀπ᾽ Οἰνόης for ἀπὸ Οἰ.; τετταράκοντα for τεσσαράκοντα

16.3 εἰς Βοῶνα for ἐς Β.; εἰς Μελάνθιον for ἐς Μ.

16.4 εἰς τὴν Ἀρητιάδα for ἐς τὴν Ἀ.; εἰς Ζεφύριον for ἐς Ζ.; εἰς τὰ Ἀργύρια for ἐς τὰ Ἀρ.

16.5 εἰς Κόραλλα for ἐς Κ.; τετταράκοντα for τεσσαράκοντα

16.6 εἰς Ἑρμώνασσαν for ἐς Ἑρμ.; τετταράκοντα for τεσσαράκοντα

17.2 εἰς ὅπερ for ἐς ὅπερ; ἐν δεξιᾷ for ἐπὶ δεξιᾷ (following P and 12.2); εἰσπλεόντων for ἐσπλ.

17.3 Roos adds τοῦ Κιμμερίου between τοῦ Βοσπόρου and πλοῦν from l; ὑπάρχοι for ὑπάρχειν (following P)

18.1 εἰς for ἐς

18.2 εἰς Ἄβασκον for ἐς Ἄβ.; ἄκραν ἔχει for ἄκρα ἀνέχει (following P and l)

18.3 εἰς Μασαϊτικὴν for ἐς Μασαϊτικήν; ἀπ᾽ Ἀχαιοῦντος for ἀπὸ δὲ Ἀχαιοῦντος (Roos adds the extra δὲ from MS l)

18.4 εἰς τὴν Παλαιὰν for ἐς τὴν Π.; εἰς Πάγρας for ἐς Π.

19.1 τετταράκοντα for τεσσαράκοντα; εἰσβάλλει for ἐσβ.; θάλατταν for θάλασσαν

19.5 εἰς Χερρόνησον for ἐς Χερ.; εἰς Κερκινῖτιν for ἐς Κ.; εἰς Καλὸν for ἐς Καλὸν

20.1 εἰς Ταμυράκην for ἐς Τ.; εἰς Ἠϊόνας for ἐς Ἠ.; εἰς ποταμὸν for ἐς ποτ.

20.2 εἰς αὐτὸν for ἐς αὐτὸν

20.3 εἰς αὐτὸν for ἐς αὐτὸν

21.1 Roos adds '[καλουμένῳ ἐς]' after ἰδίως; χροᾶς for χροιᾶς

21.2 Roos adds μὲν before ἀνατιθέναι, ἀεὶ before προσίσχουσιν, καὶ γὰρ before καὶ ἄλλα, and an extra καὶ following ἀνάκειται, all from MS p; Roos omits the second ἐν, before ἄλλῳ μέτρῳ, following MS p; ἔστι for ἔστιν

21.3 ξὺν for σὺν; θαλάττιοι for θαλάσσιοι

21.4 θεραπεύουσι for θεραπεύουσιν; θάλατταν for θάλασσαν; θαλάττης for θαλάσσης; ῥαίνουσι for ῥαίνουσιν

22.1 εἰς for ἐς

22.2 χρωμένους ἐπὶ for χρωμένους περὶ (following P)

23.1 λέγουσι for λέγουσιν; πλωϊζομένοις for πλοϊζομένοις (following Marenghi)

24.1 εἰς for ἐς; τετταράκοντα for τεσσαράκοντα

24.2 εἰς Τομέα for ἐς Τομέα

24.3 εἰς Καρῶν for ἐς Καρῶν; εἰς Τετρισιάδα for ἐς Τ.

24.4 εἰς τοῦ Αἵμου for ἐς τοῦ Αἵμου

24.6 εἰς Χερρόνησον for ἐς Χ.; εἰς Αὐλαίου for ἐς Αὐλ.; εἰς Θυνιάδα for ἐς Θ.

25.3 εἰς Κόλχους for ἐς Κ.

25.4 τετταράκοντα for τεσσαράκοντα, twice

Text and Translation

Ἀρριανοῦ
Περίπλους Εὐξείνου Πόντου

Αὐτοκράτορι Καίσαρι Τραϊανῷ Ἀδριανῷ Σεβαστῷ
Ἀρριανὸς χαίρειν.

1 Εἰς Τραπεζοῦντα ἥκομεν, πόλιν Ἑλληνίδα, ὡς λέγει ὁ
Ξενοφῶν ἐκεῖνος, ἐπὶ θαλάττῃ ᾠκισμένην, Σινωπέων
ἄποικον · καὶ τὴν μὲν θάλατταν τὴν τοῦ Εὐξείνου
ii ἄσμενοι κατείδομεν ὅθενπερ καὶ Ξενοφῶν καὶ σύ. καὶ
οἱ βωμοὶ ἀνεστᾶσιν ἤδη, λίθου μέντοι γε τοῦ τραχέος,
καὶ τὰ γράμματα διὰ τοῦτο οὐκ εὔδηλα κεχάρακται ·
τὸ δὲ Ἑλληνικὸν ἐπίγραμμα καὶ ἡμαρτημένως
γέγραπται, οἷα δὴ ὑπὸ βαρβάρων γραφέν. ἔγνωκα
οὖν τούς τε βωμοὺς λίθου λευκοῦ ἀναθεῖναι, καὶ τὰ
iii ἐπιγράμματα ἐγχαράξαι εὐσήμοις τοῖς γράμμασιν. ὁ
μὲν γὰρ ἀνδριὰς ἔστηκεν ὁ σὸς τῷ μὲν σχήματι ἡδέως
— ἀποδείκνυσι γὰρ τὴν θάλατταν — τὴν δὲ ἐργασίαν
iv οὔτε ὅμοιός σοι οὔτε ἄλλως καλός · ὥστε πέμψον
ἀνδριάντα ἄξιον ἐπονομάζεσθαι σὸν ἐν τῷ αὐτῷ
τούτῳ σχήματι · τὸ γὰρ χωρίον ἐπιτηδειότατον εἰς
μνήμην αἰώνιον.

2 Πεποίηται δὲ καὶ ὁ νεὼς λίθου τετραγώνου οὐ
φαύλως · ἀλλὰ τὸ τοῦ Ἑρμοῦ ἄγαλμα οὔτε τοῦ νεὼ
ἄξιόν ἐστιν οὔτε αὐτοῦ τοῦ χωρίου. εἰ δέ σοι δοκεῖ,
πέμψον μοι πεντάπουν μάλιστα Ἑρμοῦ ἄγαλμα —

Arrian:
Circumnavigation of the Euxine Sea

Arrian, to the Emperor Caesar Trajan Hadrian Augustus, greetings.

1 We came to Trapezous, a Greek city, as Xenophon says, founded on the sea, a colony of the Sinopeans; and gladly we looked down on the Euxine Sea from the very same spot as both

ii Xenophon and you. The altars are already set up, though in rather rough stone, and as such the inscribed letters are not particularly clear; the Greek inscription is also inaccurately carved, as it was written by barbarians. I therefore decided to rebuild the altars in white stone, and to carve the

iii inscriptions in clear letters. And though your statue has been erected in a pleasing pose – it points out to the sea – the work neither resembles

iv you nor is beautiful in any other way. So I have sent for a statue worthy to bear your name, in the same pose; for that spot is very well suited to an everlasting monument.

2 The temple has also been built in squared stone, not without care; but the image of Hermes is worthy neither of the temple nor of the place

τηλικοῦτον γάρ μοι δοκεῖ ἔσεσθαι ὥς γε πρὸς
τὸν νεὼν σύμμετρον — καὶ ἄλλο τοῦ Φιλησίου
ii τετράπουν· οὐ γὰρ ἀπὸ τρόπου δοκεῖ μοι σύνναος καὶ
σύμβωμος ἔσεσθαι τῷ προπάτορι, καὶ ὃ μέν τις τῷ
Ἑρμῇ, ὃ δὲ τῷ Φιλησίῳ, ὃ δὲ καὶ ἀμφοῖν θύσει
παριών. χαριοῦνται δὲ καὶ οὗτοι κἀκεῖνοι τῷ τε
Ἑρμῇ καὶ τῷ Φιλησίῳ· τῷ μὲν Ἑρμῇ, ὅτι τὸν
ἔγγονον αὐτοῦ τιμῶσιν, τῷ δὲ Φιλησίῳ, ὅτι τὸν
iii αὐτοῦ προπάτορα. ὡς ἔγωγε καὶ ἐβουθύτησα
ἐνταῦθα, οὐχ ὥσπερ ὁ Ξενοφῶν ἐκεῖνος ἐν Κάλπης
λιμένι ὑφ᾽ ἁμάξης βοῦν λαβὼν δι᾽ ἀπορίαν ἱερείων,
ἀλλὰ τῶν Τραπεζουντίων αὐτῶν παρασκευασάντων
ἱερεῖον οὐκ ἀγεννές. καὶ ἐσπλαγχνευσάμεθα αὐτόθι
iv καὶ ἐπὶ τοῖς σπλάγχνοις ἐπεσπείσαμεν. ὅτῳ δὲ
πρώτῳ τἀγαθὰ ηὐχόμεθα, οὐ λανθάνομέν σε τόν τε
τρόπον τὸν ἡμέτερον οὐκ ἀγνοοῦντα καὶ σαυτῷ
συνειδότα ὅτι ἄξιος εἶ ὑπὲρ ὅτου πάντες εὔξαιντο
τἀγαθὰ καὶ ὅσοι ἡμῶν ἔλαττον ὑπὸ σοῦ εὖ
πεπόνθασιν.

3 Ἐκ Τραπεζοῦντος δὲ ὁρμηθέντες τῇ μὲν πρώτῃ
εἰς Ὕσσου λιμένα κατήραμεν καὶ τοὺς πεζοὺς τοὺς
ταύτῃ ἐγυμνάσαμεν· ἡ γὰρ τάξις αὕτη, ὡς οἶσθα,
πεζῶν ἐστιν καὶ ἱππέας εἴκοσιν ὅσον εἰς διακονίαν
ἔχει· ἀλλὰ καὶ τούτους τὰς λόγχας ἀκοντίσαι
ii ἐδέησεν. ἐνθένδε ἐπλέομεν τὰ μὲν πρῶτα ταῖς αὔραις
ταῖς ἐκ τῶν ποταμῶν πνεούσαις ἕωθεν καὶ ἅμα ταῖς
κώπαις διαχρώμενοι· ψυχραὶ μὲν γὰρ ἦσαν αἱ αὖραι,
ὡς λέγει καὶ Ὅμηρος, οὐχ ἱκαναὶ δὲ τοῖς ταχυναυτεῖν
βουλομένοις. εἶτα γαλήνη ἐπέλαβεν, ὥστε καὶ ἡμεῖς
iii τῇ εἰρεσίᾳ μόνῃ ἐχρώμεθα. ἔπειτα δὲ ἄφνω νεφέλη
ἐπαναστᾶσα ἐξερράγη κατ᾽ εὖρον μάλιστα, καὶ
ἐπήνεγκεν πνεῦμα ἐξαίσιον καὶ τοῦτο ἀκριβῶς

itself. If you approve, send me a statue of Hermes about five feet tall – for that seems to me to be proportionate to the temple – and another, four
ii feet tall, of Philesios; for it is not against the custom, I think, for him to share a temple and an altar with his ancestor, and for one passer-by to sacrifice to Hermes, another to Philesios, and still another to both. All of these will gratify both Hermes and Philesios; Hermes, because they will be honouring his descendant, and Philesios, his
iii ancestor. I also sacrificed an ox there – not like Xenophon in Kalpes Limen (who, lacking animals for sacrifice, took an ox from a chariot), as I had been provided an ox of not ignoble stock by the Trapezuntines – and we examined the entrails, and
iv poured a libation on them. We did not forget that you, for whose well-being we first offered prayers, are aware of our custom, and that you know yourself to be worthy of prayers from all, including those who have benefited less from you than I have, for your prosperity.

3 Having set off from Trapezus, we put into Hyssou Limen on the first day and exercised the infantry there. That cohort of foot-soldiers, as you know, also has 20 cavalry, which is sufficient;
ii we also made them throw their javelins. From there at first we sailed with the winds that blow from the rivers in the morning and at the same time used the oars; for the winds were cold, as Homer once said, but were not strong enough for those who want to sail quickly. Soon a calm took
iii hold, so we too just rowed. Then suddenly clouds

ἐναντίον, ὅπερ καὶ μόνον ὤνησεν ἡμᾶς · κοίλην μὲν
γὰρ δι᾽ ὀλίγου τὴν θάλατταν ἐποίησεν, ὡς μὴ κατὰ
τὰς κώπας μόνον ἀλλὰ καὶ ὑπὲρ τὰς παρεξειρεσίας
ἐπεισρεῖν ἡμῖν ἑκατέρωθεν ἀφθόνως τοῦ ὕδατος,
iv τοῦτο δὴ τὸ τραγικόν,

καὶ τὴν μὲν ἐξηντλοῦμεν, ἣ δ᾽ ἐπεισέρρει.

ἀλλ᾽ οὐ πλάγιόν γε ἦν τὸ κλυδώνιον. ταύτῃ καὶ
ἠνύτομεν μόγις καὶ χαλεπῶς τῇ εἰρεσίᾳ, καὶ μέντοι
πολλὰ παθόντες ἥκομεν εἰς τὰς Ἀθήνας.
4 Ἔστι γάρ τοι καὶ ἐν Πόντῳ τῷ Εὐξείνῳ χωρίον
οὕτω καλούμενον, καί τι καὶ Ἀθηνᾶς ἱερόν ἐστιν
αὐτόθι Ἑλληνικόν, ὅθεν μοι δοκεῖ καὶ τὸ ὄνομα εἶναι
τοῦτο τῷ χωρίῳ, καὶ φρούριόν τι ἐστὶν ἠμελημένον.
ii ὁ δὲ ὅρμος οἷος ὥρᾳ ἔτους δέχεσθαι οὐ πολλὰς ναῦς
καὶ σκέπην ταύταις παρέχειν ἀπὸ νότου ἀνέμου καὶ
αὐτοῦ τοῦ εὔρου · σῴζοιτο δ᾽ ἂν καὶ τοῦ βορρᾶ τὰ
ὁρμοῦντα πλοῖα, ἀλλ᾽ οὐ τοῦ γε ἀπαρκίου οὐδὲ τοῦ
θρασκίου μὲν ἐν τῷ Πόντῳ, σκίρωνος δὲ ἐν τῇ
iii Ἑλλάδι καλουμένου. εἰς δὲ τὴν νύκτα βρονταί τε
σκληραὶ καὶ ἀστραπαὶ κατεῖχον, καὶ πνεῦμα οὐ τὸ
αὐτὸ ἔτι, ἀλλ᾽ εἰς νότον μεθειστήκει, καὶ δι᾽ ὀλίγου
ἀπὸ τοῦ νότου εἰς λίβα ἄνεμον, καὶ ταῖς ναυσὶν
iv οὐκέτι ἀσφαλὴς ὁ ὅρμος ἦν. πρὶν οὖν παντάπασιν
ἀγριωθῆναι τὴν θάλατταν, ὅσας μὲν αὐτὸ τὸ χωρίον
αἱ Ἀθῆναι δέξασθαι ἠδύναντο, ταύτας αὐτοῦ
ἐνεωλκήσαμεν, πλὴν τῆς τριήρους · αὕτη γὰρ πέτρᾳ
τινὶ ὑφορμοῦσα ἀσφαλῶς ἐσάλευεν.
5 Τὰς δὲ πολλὰς ἐδόκει πέμπειν εἰς τοὺς αἰγιαλοὺς
τοὺς πλησίον νεωλκηθησομένας. καὶ ἐνεωλκήθησαν
ὥστε ἀπαθεῖς διαγενέσθαι πάσας πλὴν μιᾶς, ἥντινα ἐν
τῷ ὁρμίζεσθαι πρὸ τοῦ καιροῦ ἐπιστρέψασαν πλαγίαν

rose up and broke out from the east, and a violent wind
came upon us from exactly the opposite direction,
which was the only thing that helped us, as for a short
while it made a hollow in the sea, without which we
would have been swamped with plenty of water from
both sides, not only over the oars but even over the
v   decks too. Just as in that tragic verse

We baled it out, but it still rushed in;

but the surf did not come over the sides. So we
made our way with difficulty by rowing: but at last,
having suffered much, we arrived at Athenai.

4   For there is in the Euxine Sea a place so named,
and there, there is a Greek temple of Athena from
which I imagine the place got that name, and also an
ii   abandoned fort. The mooring at the right time of year
can accommodate a few ships and shelters them from
the south wind, and even the east; it may also save
moored ships from the north wind, but not from the
Aparktias, nor from the wind called the Thraskian in
iii   the Euxine Sea, and the Skironian in Greece. At night
came violent thunder, and lightning too; the wind was
not constant, but turned to the south, and after a while
from the south to the south west, and the mooring was
iv   no longer safe for the ships. Therefore, before the sea
turned completely savage, we beached all the ships
that that place Athenai could hold, except the trireme;
for that, moored up by a rock, safely rode at anchor.

5   I decided to send the large ships to the
neighbouring coast to be beached. They were
beached so that they all came through unscathed
except one, which, its side having turned in the

ὑπολαβὸν τὸ κῦμα ἐξήνεγκεν εἰς τὴν ἠϊόνα καὶ
ii συνέτριψεν. ἀπεσώθη μέντοι πάντα, οὐ τὰ ἱστία
μόνον καὶ τὰ σκεύη τὰ ναυτικὰ καὶ οἱ ἄνθρωποι, ἀλλὰ
καὶ οἱ ἧλοι, καὶ ὁ κηρὸς ἀπεξύσθη, ὡς μηδενὸς ἄλλου
ἢ ξύλων δεῖσθαι ναυπηγησίμων εἰς τὴν κατασκευήν,
ὧν παμπόλλη, ὡς οἶσθα, ἀφθονία ἐστὶν κατὰ τὸν
iii Πόντον. οὗτος ὁ χειμὼν ἐπὶ δύο ἡμέρας κατεῖχεν,
καὶ ἦν ἀνάγκη μένειν. ἐχρῆν γὰρ ἄρα μηδὲ τὰς ἐν τῷ
Πόντῳ Ἀθήνας παραπλεῦσαι ἡμᾶς ὥσπερ τινὰ ὅρμον
ἔρημον καὶ ἀνώνυμον.
6 Ἐνθένδε ἄραντες ὑπὸ μὲν τὴν ἔω πλαγίου τοῦ
κλύδωνος ἐπειρώμεθα, προϊούσης δὲ τῆς ἡμέρας
βορρᾶς ἐπιπνεύσας ὀλίγος κατέστησε τὴν θάλατταν
καὶ διατρεμῆσαι ἐποίησεν. καὶ ἤλθομεν πρὸ τῆς
μεσημβρίας σταδίους πλείονας ἢ πεντ[ήκοντα καὶ
δι]ακοσίους εἰς Ἄψαρον, ἵναπερ αἱ πέντε σπεῖραί εἰσιν
ii ἱδρυμέναι. καὶ τὴν μισθοφορὰν τῇ στρατιᾷ ἔδωκα
καὶ τὰ ὅπλα εἶδον καὶ τὸ τεῖχος καὶ τὴν τάφρον καὶ
τοὺς κάμνοντας καὶ τοῦ σίτου τὴν παρασκευὴν τὴν
ἐνοῦσαν. ἥντινα δὲ ὑπὲρ αὐτῶν τὴν γνώμην ἔσχον,
iii ἐν τοῖς Ῥωμαϊκοῖς γράμμασιν γέγραπται. ὁ δὲ
Ἄψαρος τὸ χωρίον λέγουσιν ὅτι Ἄψυρτος
ἐκαλεῖτο πάλαι ποτέ · ἐνταῦθα γὰρ τὸν Ἄψυρτον ὑπὸ
τῆς Μηδείας ἀποθανεῖν, καὶ τάφος Ἀψύρτου
δείκνυται. ἔπειτα διαφθαρῆναι τοὔνομα ὑπὸ τῶν
περιοίκων βαρβάρων, καθάπερ καὶ ἄλλα πολλὰ
iv διέφθαρται · ὁπότε καὶ τὰ Τύανα τὰ ἐν τοῖς
Καππαδόκαις Θόανα λέγουσιν ὅτι ὠνομάζετο ἐπὶ
Θόαντι τῷ βασιλεῖ τῶν Ταύρων, ὃς τοὺς ἀμφὶ
Ὀρέστην καὶ Πυλάδην διώκων ἄχρι τῆσδε τῆς χώρας
ἐλθεῖν φημίζεται καὶ ἐνταῦθα νόσῳ ἀποθανεῖν.

mooring too early, was taken up by a wave and
ii   dashed against the shore, and broken up.
Everything was rescued, though; not only the sail,
the rigging, and the men, but also the nails and
sealing-wax were stripped off, so that nothing of
the fittings remained but the ship's timber, of
which, as you know, there is a great abundance in
iii the Euxine.   The storm lasted two days, and
forced us to stay there.   And thus we could not
sail past Athenai in the Euxine like some
deserted and nameless anchorage.

6   Having weighed anchor from there towards
morning we did battle with the waves coming
over the sides, but the following day a light
northerly wind blew down and steadied the sea
and made it thoroughly calm. And before midday
we came more than [2]50 stades to Apsaros, where
ii   the five cohorts are stationed. I gave the army its
pay and inspected its weapons, the walls, the
trench, the sick, and the food supplies that were
there.   My opinion about this latter point I have
iii written to you in the Latin report. It is said that
Apsaros was once called Apsyrtos; for it was there
that Apsyrtos was killed by Medea, and the tomb
of Apsyrtos is on show.   The name was
subsequently corrupted by the barbarians who
live around there, just as many others were
iv   corrupted too; since they say that Tyana in
Cappadocia was named Thoana after Thoas, king
of the Tauroi, who, while pursuing Orestes and
Pylades, is said to have come as far as this region
and to have died here of a disease.

7   Ποταμοὺς δὲ παρημείψαμεν ἐν τῷ παράπλῳ τῷ
ἀπὸ Τραπεζοῦντος τόν τε Ὕσσον, ὅτου ἐπώνυμος
Ὕσσου λιμήν, ὃς ἀπέχει Τραπεζοῦντος σταδίους
ὀγδοήκοντα καὶ ἑκατόν, καὶ τὸν Ὄφιν, ὃς ἀπέχει
Ὕσσου λιμένος εἰς ἐνενήκοντα σταδίους μάλιστα καὶ
ii   ὁρίζει τὴν Κόλχων χώραν ἀπὸ τῆς Θιαννικῆς. ἔπειτα
τὸν Ψυχρὸν καλούμενον ποταμὸν διέχοντα ὅσον
τριάκοντα σταδίους ἀπὸ τοῦ Ὄφεως. ἔπειτα τὸν
Καλὸν ποταμόν · καὶ οὗτος τριάκοντα διέχει ἀπὸ τοῦ
Ψυχροῦ. ἐχόμενος δὲ τοῦ Ψυχροῦ ἐστιν ὁ Ῥίζιος
ποταμός, ἑκατὸν εἴκοσι στάδια διέχων ἀπὸ τοῦ
iii Καλοῦ. καὶ ἀπὸ τούτου τριάκοντα Ἄσκουρος ἄλλος
ποταμός, καὶ Ἀδιηνός τις ἀπὸ τοῦ Ἀσκούρου
ἑξήκοντα · ἐνθένδε εἰς Ἀθήνας ὀγδοήκοντα καὶ
ἑκατόν. ταῖς δὲ Ἀθήναις Ζάγατις ποταμὸς ἑπτὰ
μάλιστα στάδια ἀπ' αὐτῶν διέχων πρόσκειται. ἀπὸ
δὲ τῶν Ἀθηνῶν ὁρμηθέντες τὸν Πρύτανιν
παρημείψαμεν, ἵναπερ καὶ τὰ Ἀγχιάλου βασίλειά
ἐστιν. καὶ οὗτος ἀπέχει τετταράκοντα στάδια ἀπὸ
iv   τῶν Ἀθηνῶν. τοῦ Πρυτάνεως δὲ ἔχεται ὁ Πυξίτης
ποταμός · στάδιοι ἐνενήκοντα ἐν μέσῳ ἀμφοῖν. καὶ
ἀπὸ τοῦ Πυξίτου εἰς Ἄρχαβιν ἄλλοι ἐνενήκοντα, ἀπὸ
δὲ Ἀρχάβιος εἰς Ἄψαρον ἑξήκοντα. ἀπὸ δὲ Ἀψάρου
ἄραντες τὸν Ἄκαμψιν παρημείψαμεν νύκτωρ, εἰς
v   πεντεκαίδεκα σταδίους ἀπέχοντα τοῦ Ἀψάρου. ὁ δὲ
Βαθὺς ποταμὸς ἑβδομήκοντα καὶ πέντε ἀπέχει
τούτου, καὶ ὁ Ἀκινάσης ἀπὸ τοῦ Βαθέος ἐνενήκοντα,
ἐνενήκοντα δὲ καὶ ἀπ' Ἀκινάσου ὁ Ἶσις. ναυσίποροι
δέ εἰσιν ὅ τε Ἄκαμψις καὶ ὁ Ἶσις, καὶ αὔρας τὰς
ἑωθινὰς ἰσχυρὰς ἐκπέμπουσιν. ἀπὸ δὲ Ἴσιος τὸν
Μῶγρον παρημείψαμεν. ἐνενήκοντα στάδιοι μεταξὺ

7 The rivers we passed on our voyage from
Trapezus were the Hyssos, after which Hyssou
Limen is named, and which is 180 stades from
Trapezus, and the Ophis, which is about 90
stades from Hyssos harbour and separates the
territory of Colchis from that of Thiannike.

ii Then the river called Psychros, around about 30
stades from the Ophis. Then the Kalos river; this
one too is 30 stades distant from the Psychros.
Coming next to the Psychros is the Rhizios river,

iii 120 stades distant from the Kalos. And 30 after
this comes another river, the Askouros, and the
Adienos 60 after the Askouros; then it is 180 to
Athenai. The river Zagatis lies near Athenai,
about 7 stades distant from it. From our mooring
at Athenai we passed by the Prytanis, where
Anchialos' palace is. And that is 40 stades

iv distant from Athenai. The Pyxites river is the
Prytanis' neighbour; there are 90 stades between
the two. And from the Pyxites to the Archabis is
another 90, and from the Archabis to Apsaros, 60.
Weighing anchor from Apsaros we passed by the
Akampsis by night, 15 stades distant from Apsaros.

v The river Bathys is 75 distant from there, and the
Akinases 90 from the Bathys, and the Isis 90
from the Akinases. Both the Akampsis and the
Isis are navigable, and send down strong winds in
the morning. From the Isis we passed by the
Mogros; there are 90 stades between the Mogros
and the Isis. It too is navigable.

τοῦ Μώγρου εἰσὶν καὶ τοῦ Ἴσιος. καὶ οὗτος ναυσίπορος.

8　Ἐνθένδε εἰς τὸν Φᾶσιν εἰσεπλεύσαμεν ἐνενήκοντα τοῦ Μώγρου διέχοντα, ποταμῶν ὧν ἐγὼ ἔγνων κουφότατον ὕδωρ παρεχόμενον καὶ τὴν χρόαν μάλιστα
ii　ἐξηλλαγμένον. τὴν μὲν γὰρ κουφότητα τῷ τε σταθμῷ τεκμαίροιτο ἄν τις, καὶ πρὸ τούτου, ὅτι ἐπιπλεῖ τῇ θαλάττῃ, οὐχὶ δὲ συμμίγνυται, καθάπερ τῷ Πηνειῷ τὸν Τιταρήσιον λέγει ἐπιρρεῖν Ὅμηρος
iii　καθύπερθεν ἠΰτ' ἔλαιον. καὶ ἦν κατὰ μὲν τοῦ ἐπιρρέοντος βάψαντα γλυκὺ τὸ ὕδωρ ἀνιμήσασθαι, εἰ δὲ εἰς βάθος τις καθῆκεν τὴν κάλπιν, ἁλμυρόν. καίτοι ὁ πᾶς Πόντος πολύ τι γλυκυτέρου τοῦ ὕδατός ἐστιν ἤπερ ἡ ἔξω θάλαττα· καὶ τούτου τὸ αἴτιον οἱ ποταμοί εἰσιν, οὔτε πλῆθος οὔτε μέγεθος σταθμητοὶ
iv　ὄντες. τεκμήριον δὲ τῆς γλυκύτητος, εἰ τεκμηρίων δεῖ ἐπὶ τοῖς αἰσθήσει φαινομένοις, ὅτι πάντα τὰ βοσκήματα οἱ προσοικοῦντες τῇ θαλάττῃ ἐπὶ τὴν θάλατταν κατάγουσιν καὶ ἀπ' αὐτῆς ποτίζουσιν· τὰ δὲ πίνοντά τε ἡδέως ὁρᾶται, καὶ λόγος κατέχει ὅτι καὶ ὠφέλιμον αὐτοῖς τοῦτο τὸ ποτόν ἐστιν τοῦ
v　γλυκέος μᾶλλον. ἡ δὲ χρόα τῷ Φάσιδι οἷα ἀπὸ μολίβδου ἢ καττιτέρου βεβαμμένου τοῦ ὕδατος· καταστὰν δὲ καθαρώτατον γίγνεται. οὐ τοίνυν νενόμισται εἰσκομίσαι ὕδωρ εἰς τὸν Φᾶσιν τοὺς εἰσπλέοντας, ἀλλ' ἐπειδὰν εἰσβαίνωσιν ἤδη εἰς τὸν ῥοῦν, παραγγέλλεται πᾶν ἐκχέαι τὸ ἐνὸν ὕδωρ ἐν ταῖς ναυσίν· εἰ δὲ μή, λόγος κατέχει ὅτι οἱ τούτου ἀμελήσαντες οὐκ εὐπλοοῦσιν. τὸ δὲ ὕδωρ τοῦ Φάσιδος οὐ σήπεται, ἀλλὰ μένει ἀκραιφνὲς καὶ ὑπὲρ δέκατον ἔτος, πλήν γε δὴ ὅτι εἰς τὸ γλυκύτερον μεταβάλλει.

8   From there, we sailed into the Phasis, 90 stades
     from the Mogros, which supplies the lightest and
     the strangest-coloured water of any of the rivers I
ii   know. One may judge its lightness by means of a
     balance, and, more immediately, by the fact that
     it floats on the sea, not mixing with it, just as
     Homer said of the Titaresus, that floats 'on top of'
iii the Peneus 'like oil'. Indeed, if one should dip just
     beneath the surface, it is possible to draw out
     fresh water, but then, by sinking the cup deeper,
     to draw out salty water. Moreover, the whole
     Pontus has much fresher water than the sea
     outside it; the reason for this is its rivers, being so
iv   many and so great in volume. The proof of this
     freshness – if proof of perceptible phenomena be
     necessary – is that those who live around the sea
     lead all their cattle down to the sea and water
     them from it; they seem to drink happily, and the
     opinion is that this watering spot is more beneficial
v   to them than fresh water is. The colour of the
     Phasis is that of water that has been tainted with
     lead or tin; but, being left to stand, it becomes
     extremely clear. Furthermore, those who sail in
     are traditionally forbidden from importing water
     into the Phasis, and as soon as they enter its
     stream they are ordered to pour out all water
     from outside that is on the ships. Those
     neglecting to do so, it is said, will not otherwise
     sail on favourably. And the water of the Phasis
     does not stagnate, but remains unchanged for
     upwards of ten years – if anything, it becomes
     fresher.

9 Εἰσβαλλόντων δὲ εἰς τὸν Φᾶσιν ἐν ἀριστερᾷ ἵδρυται ἡ Φασιανὴ θεός. εἴη δ᾽ ἂν ἀπό γε τοῦ σχήματος τεκμαιρομένῳ ἡ Ῥέα· καὶ γὰρ κύμβαλον μετὰ χεῖρας ἔχει καὶ λέοντας ὑπὸ τῷ θρόνῳ, καὶ κάθηται ὥσπερ ἐν τῷ Μητρῴῳ Ἀθήνησιν ἡ τοῦ Φειδίου. ἐνταῦθα καὶ

ii ἡ ἄγκυρα δείκνυται τῆς Ἀργοῦς. καὶ ἡ μὲν σιδηρᾶ οὐκ ἔδοξέ μοι εἶναι παλαιά — καίτοι τὸ μέγεθος οὐ κατὰ τὰς νῦν ἀγκύρας ἐστίν, καὶ τὸ σχῆμα ἀμηγέπη ἐξηλλαγμένη — ἀλλὰ νεωτέρα μοι ἐφάνη εἶναι τοῦ χρόνου. λιθίνης δέ τινος ἄλλης θραύσματα ἐδείκνυτο παλαιά, ὡς ταῦτα μᾶλλον εἰκάσαι ἐκεῖνα εἶναι τὰ λείψανα τῆς ἀγκύρας τῆς Ἀργοῦς. ἄλλο δὲ οὐδὲν ὑπόμνημα ἦν ἐνταῦθα τῶν μύθων τῶν ἀμφὶ τὸν

iii Ἰάσονα. τὸ μέντοι φρούριον αὐτό, ἵναπερ κάθηνται τετρακόσιοι στρατιῶται ἐπίλεκτοι, τῇ τε φύσει τοῦ χωρίου ὀχυρώτατον εἶναί μοι ἔδοξεν, καὶ ἐν ἐπιτηδειοτάτῳ κεῖσθαι πρὸς ἀσφάλειαν τῶν ταύτῃ πλεόντων. καὶ τάφρος διπλῆ περιβέβληται τῷ τείχει,

iv εὐρεῖα ἑκατέρα. πάλαι μὲν οὖν γήϊνον τὸ τεῖχος ἦν, καὶ οἱ πύργοι ξύλινοι ἐφειστήκεσαν· νῦν δὲ ἐκ πλίνθου ὀπτῆς πεποίηται καὶ αὐτὸ καὶ οἱ πύργοι· καὶ τεθεμελίωται ἀσφαλῶς, καὶ μηχαναὶ ἐφεστᾶσιν, καὶ ἐν ὀλίγῳ πᾶσιν ἐξήρτυται πρὸς τὸ μηδὲ πελάσαι ἄν τινα αὐτῷ τῶν βαρβάρων, μήτι γε δὴ εἰς κίνδυνον καταστῆσαι πολιορκίας τοὺς ἐν αὐτῷ φρουροῦντας.

v ἐπειδὴ δὲ καὶ τὸν ὅρμον ἐχρῆν ἀσφαλῆ εἶναι ταῖς ναυσὶ καὶ ὅσα ἔξω τοῦ φρουρίου κατῳκεῖτο ὑπό τε τῶν πεπαυμένων τῆς στρατιᾶς καί τινων καὶ ἄλλων ἐμπορικῶν ἀνθρώπων, ἔδοξέ μοι ἀπὸ τῆς διπλῆς τάφρου, ἣ περιβέβληται τῷ τείχει, ἄλλην τάφρον ἐκβαλεῖν ὡς ἐπὶ τὸν ποταμόν, ἣ τό τε ναύσταθμον περιέξει καὶ τὰς ἔξω τοῦ τείχους οἰκίας.

9   On the left-hand side of one entering the Phasis
sits the goddess Phasiane.   Judging by her
attributes, she is Rhea; for she has a cymbal in
her hand and lions beneath her throne, and
sits just like the one by Phidias in the Athenian
ii Metroön.   Here too is displayed the anchor
from the *Argo*. This object, made of iron, does not
look old to me – although it is not the size of
modern anchors, and the shape has been altered
in some way – but appears to be more recent. But
also on display are some old fragments of a stone
one, and it is rather these, one would guess,
which are the remains of the anchor of the *Argo*.
But there is no other monument there to the
iii legends about Jason.   In any case, the fort itself,
in which 400 select troops are quartered, seemed
to me, owing to the nature of its site, to be very
secure, and to lie in the most convenient spot for
the safety of those who sail this way.   In addition,
a double ditch has been put round the wall, each
iv ditch as broad as the other.   The wall used to be
of earth, and wooden towers were set up above it;
now both it and the towers are made of baked
brick.   And its foundations are firm, and war
engines are installed – and in short, it is fully
equipped to prevent any of the barbarians
from even approaching it, let alone to protect the
v garrison there against the danger of a siege.   But
since the mooring-place for the ships must also be
secure, as well as the whole area outside the fort
settled by veterans of the army, various
merchants and others, I decided to construct

10 Ἀπὸ δὲ τοῦ Φάσιδος Χαρίεντα ποταμὸν
παρημείψαμεν ναυσίπορον· στάδιοι μεταξὺ ἀμφοῖν
ἐνενήκοντα. καὶ ἀπὸ τοῦ Χαρίεντος εἰς Χῶβον
ποταμὸν εἰσεπλεύσαμεν ἄλλους ἐνενήκοντα, ἵναπερ
καὶ ὡρμίσθημεν. ὧν δὲ ἕνεκα, καὶ ὅσα ἐνταῦθα
ἐπράξαμεν, δηλώσει σοι τὰ Ῥωμαϊκὰ γράμματα.

ii ἀπὸ δὲ Χώβου Σιγάμην ποταμὸν παρημείψαμεν
ναυσίπορον· διέχει δὲ τοῦ Χώβου σταδίους εἰς δέκα
καὶ διακοσίους μάλιστα. ἔχεται δὲ τοῦ Σιγάμου
Ταρσούρας ποταμός· στάδιοι εἴκοσι καὶ ἑκατὸν
μεταξὺ ἀμφοῖν. ὁ δὲ Ἵππος ποταμὸς τοῦ Ταρσούρου
πεντήκοντα σταδίους καὶ ἑκατὸν διέχει, καὶ τοῦ

iii Ἵππου ὁ Ἀστέλεφος τριάκοντα. παραμείψαντες δὲ
τὸν Ἀστέλεφον εἰς Σεβαστόπολιν ἥκομεν πρὸ
μεσημβρίας, ἀπὸ Χώβου ὁρμηθέντες, σταδίους εἴκοσι
καὶ ἑκατὸν τοὺς ἀπ᾽ Ἀστελέφου, ὡς καὶ τὴν
μισθοφορὰν τοῖς στρατιώταις δοῦναι τῆς αὐτῆς
ἡμέρας, καὶ τοὺς ἵππους καὶ τὰ ὅπλα ἰδεῖν καὶ τοὺς
ἱππέας ἀναπηδῶντας ἐπὶ τοὺς ἵππους καὶ τοὺς
κάμνοντας καὶ τὸν σῖτον, καὶ τὸ τεῖχος περιελθεῖν καὶ

iv τὴν τάφρον. στάδιοι ἀπὸ μὲν Χώβου εἰς Σεβαστόπολιν
τριάκοντα καὶ ἑξακόσιοι· ἀπὸ Τραπεζοῦντος δὲ εἰς
Σεβαστόπολιν ἑξήκοντα καὶ διακόσιοι καὶ δισχίλιοι.
ἡ δὲ Σεβαστόπολις πάλαι Διοσκουριὰς ἐκαλεῖτο,
ἄποικος Μιλησίων.

11 Ἔθνη δὲ παρημείψαμεν τάδε. Τραπεζουντίοις μέν,
καθάπερ καὶ Ξενοφῶν λέγει, Κόλχοι ὅμοροι. καὶ οὓς
λέγει τοὺς μαχιμωτάτους καὶ ἐχθροτάτους εἶναι τοῖς
Τραπεζουντίοις, ἐκεῖνος μὲν Δρίλλας ὀνομάζει, ἐμοὶ
δὲ δοκοῦσιν οἱ Σάννοι οὗτοι εἶναι. καὶ γὰρ
μαχιμώτατοί εἰσιν εἰς τοῦτο ἔτι καὶ τοῖς Τραπεζουντίοις

ii ἐχθρότατοι, καὶ χωρία ὀχυρὰ οἰκοῦσιν, καὶ ἔθνος

another ditch from the double ditch that surrounds the wall as far as the river, which would enclose both the harbour and the houses outside the walls.

10 From the Phasis, we passed the navigable river Charies; there are 90 stades between the two. From the Charies, we sailed on another 90 stades to the river Chobos, and there we anchored. The reason for this, and what we did there, my letter

ii in Latin will explain to you. From the Chobos, we passed the navigable river Sigame; it is approximately 210 stades from the Chobos. After the Sigame is the river Tarsouras; there are 120 stades between the two. The river Hippos is 150 stades beyond the Tarsouras, and the

iii Astelephos 30 beyond the Hippos. Leaving behind the Astelephos, we came to Sebastopolis before midday, having set out from the Chobos and having done 120 stades since the Astelephos, so that we could give the soldiers the same day's pay, and inspect the horses and weapons, the horsemen leaping on to their mounts, the sick and the supplies, and also make a tour of the wall

iv and the ditch. It is 630 stades from the Chobos to Sebastopolis; from Trapezous to Sebastopolis it is 2,260. Sebastopolis used to be called Dioskourias, and is a colony of the Milesians.

11 We passed by the following peoples. The Colchoi border on the Trapezuntines, just as Xenophon says. And the people he records as being most warlike and hostile towards the Trapezuntines, he calls Drillai, but I think they

ἀβασίλευτον, πάλαι μὲν καὶ φόρου ὑποτελὲς
Ῥωμαίοις, ὑπὸ δὲ τοῦ ληστεύειν οὐκ ἀκριβοῦσιν τὴν
φοράν. ἀλλὰ νῦν γε διδόντος θεοῦ ἀκριβώσουσιν, ἢ
ἐξελοῦμεν αὐτούς. τούτων δὲ ἔχονται Μαχέλονες καὶ
Ἡνίοχοι · βασιλεὺς δ' αὐτῶν Ἀγχίαλος. Μαχελόνων
δὲ καὶ Ἡνιόχων ἐχόμενοι Ζυδρεῖται · Φαρασμάνου
οὗτοι ὑπήκοοι. Ζυδρειτῶν δὲ Λαζοί · βασιλεὺς δὲ
iii Λαζῶν Μαλάσσας, ὃς τὴν βασιλείαν παρὰ σοῦ ἔχει.
Λαζῶν δὲ Ἀψίλαι ἔχονται· βασιλεὺς δ' αὐτῶν
Ἰουλιανός · οὗτος ἐκ τοῦ πατρὸς τοῦ σοῦ τὴν
βασιλείαν ἔχει. Ἀψίλαις δὲ ὅμοροι Ἀβασκοί ·
καὶ Ἀβασκῶν βασιλεὺς Ῥησμάγας · καὶ οὗτος παρὰ
σοῦ τὴν βασιλείαν ἔχει. Ἀβασκῶν δὲ ἐχόμενοι
Σανίγαι, ἵναπερ καὶ ἡ Σεβαστόπολις ᾤκισται ·
Σανιγῶν βασιλεὺς Σπαδάγας ἐκ σοῦ τὴν
βασιλείαν ἔχει.
iv Μέχρι μὲν δὴ Ἀψάρου ὡς πρὸς ἕω ἐπλέομεν ἐν
δεξιᾷ τοῦ Εὐξείνου, ὁ δὲ Ἄψαρος πέρας ἐφάνη μοι
εἶναι κατὰ μῆκος τοῦ Πόντου · ἔνθεν γὰρ ἤδη πρὸς
ἄρκτον ὁ πλοῦς ἡμῖν ἐγίνετο ἔστε ἐπὶ Χῶβον
ποταμόν, καὶ ὑπὲρ τὸν Χῶβον ἐπὶ τὸν Σιγάμην. ἀπὸ
δὲ Σιγάμου ἐκάμπτομεν εἰς τὴν λαιὰν πλευρὰν τοῦ
v Πόντου ἔστε ἐπὶ τὸν Ἵππον ποταμόν. ἀπὸ δὲ τοῦ
Ἵππου ὡς ἐπ' Ἀστέλεφον καὶ Διοσκουριάδα
κατ[αφανῶς ἤδη ἐπ' ἀριστερὰ τοῦ Πόντου ἐπλέομεν,
καὶ ὁ πλοῦς ἡμῖν πρὸς ἡλίου δυομένου ἐγίνετο · ὡς δὲ
ὑπεστρέφομεν ἀπὸ τοῦ Ἀστελέφου ἐπὶ Διοσκουριάδα
κατ]είδομεν τὸν Καύκασον τὸ ὄρος, τὸ ὕψος μάλιστα
κατὰ τὰς Ἄλπεις τὰς Κελτικάς. καὶ τοῦ Καυκάσου
κορυφή τις ἐδείκνυτο — Στρόβιλος τῇ κορυφῇ ὄνομα
— ἵναπερ ὁ Προμηθεὺς κρεμασθῆναι ὑφ' Ἡφαίστου
κατὰ πρόσταξιν Διὸς μυθεύεται.

are actually Sannoi. For they too are very warlike,
ii even to this day, and are hostile to the Trapezuntines,
live in fortified places, and are a tribe without a king.
They were also formerly liable for tribute to the
Romans, although, being pirates, they are not anxious
to pay their tribute. But nowadays, God willing, they
will be, or we will exterminate them. After them come
the Machelones and the Heniochoi; their king is
Anchialos. Coming after the Machelones and the
Heniochoi are the Zydritai; they are subject to
Pharasmanes. After the Zydritai are the Lazoi; the
king of the Lazoi is Malassas, who holds his kingdom
iii from you. After the Lazoi come the Apsilai; their king
is Julianus, and he holds his kingdom from your father.
The Abascoi border on the Apsilai; the king of the
Abasci is Rhesmagas, and he holds his kingdom from
you. After the Abascoi come the Sanigai, in whose
territory Sebastopolis was founded: the king of the
Sanigai is Spadagas, who holds his kingdom from you.

iv   As far as Apsaros we were sailing eastwards, in the
right-hand part of the Euxine, and Apsaros seemed to
me to be the limit of the length of the Pontus; for from
there our voyage was northwards as far as the river
Chobos, and beyond the Chobos to the Sigames. From
the Sigames we veered towards the left-hand flank of
the Pontus as far as the river Hippos. From the
Hippos to the Astelephos and Dioskourias, we [sailed
directly towards the left of the Pontus, and our voyage
was into the setting sun; then, turning from the
Astelephos towards Dioskourias, we] saw the Caucasus
mountain, which is just as high as the Celtic Alps. And
the summit of the Caucasus – which is called Strobilos

12 Τὰ δὲ ἀπὸ Βοσπόρου τοῦ Θρᾳκίου ἔστε ἐπὶ Τραπεζοῦντα
ii πόλιν ὧδε ἔχει. τὸ ἱερὸν τοῦ Διὸς τοῦ Οὐρίου διέχει
ἀπὸ Βυζαντίου σταδίους εἴκοσι καὶ ἑκατόν, καί ἐστι
στενότατον ταύτῃ τὸ στόμα τοῦ Πόντου καλούμενον,
καθ' ὅ τι εἰσβάλλει εἰς τὴν Προποντίδα. ταῦτα μὲν
iii εἰδότι σοι λέγω. ἀπὸ δὲ τοῦ Ἱεροῦ πλέοντι ἐν δεξιᾷ
Ῥήβας ποταμός · σταδίους διέχει τοῦ Ἱεροῦ τοῦ Διὸς
ἐνενήκοντα. ἔπειτα Μέλαινα ἄκρα ὧδε καλουμένη,
πεντήκοντα καὶ ἑκατόν. ἀπὸ Μελαίνης ἄκρας εἰς
Ἀρτάνην ποταμόν, ἵνα καὶ ὅρμος ναυσὶ μικραῖς πρὸς
iv ἱερῷ Ἀφροδίτης, πεντήκοντα ἄλλοι καὶ ἑκατόν. ἀπὸ
δὲ Ἀρτάνης εἰς Ψίλιν ποταμὸν πεντήκοντα καὶ
ἑκατόν · καὶ πλοῖα μικρὰ ὁρμίζοιτο ἂν πρὸς τῇ
πέτρᾳ τῇ ἀνεχούσῃ οὐ πόρρω ἀπὸ τοῦ ποταμοῦ
τῶν ἐκβολῶν. ἐνθένδε εἰς Κάλπης λιμένα δέκα καὶ
v διακόσιοι στάδιοι. ὁ δὲ Κάλπης λιμὴν ὁποῖόν τι
χωρίον ἐστὶ καὶ ὁποῖος ὅρμος, καὶ ὅτι πηγὴ ἐν αὐτῷ
ψυχροῦ καὶ καθαροῦ ὕδατος, καὶ ὅτι ὗλαι πρὸς τῇ
θαλάττῃ ξύλων ναυπηγησίμων, καὶ αὗται ἔνθηροι,
ταῦτα Ξενοφῶντι τῷ πρεσβυτέρῳ λέλεκται.

13 Ἀπὸ Κάλπης λιμένος εἰς Ῥόην στάδιοι εἴκοσιν ·
ὅρμος ναυσὶ μικραῖς. ἀπὸ Ῥόης εἰς Ἀπολλωνίαν
νῆσον σμικράν, ὀλίγον διέχουσαν τῆς ἠπείρου, ἄλλοι
εἴκοσι. λιμὴν ὑπὸ τῇ νησῖδι. καὶ ἔνθεν εἰς Χηλὰς
στάδιοι εἴκοσιν. ἀπὸ Χηλῶν ὀγδοήκοντα καὶ ἑκατόν,
ἵναπερ Σαγγάριος ποταμὸς εἰσβάλλει εἰς τὸν Πόντον.
ii ἐνθένδε εἰς τοῦ Ὑπίου τὰς ἐκβολὰς ἄλλοι ὀγδοήκοντα
καὶ ἑκατόν. εἰς δὲ Λιλαῖον ἐμπόριον ἀπὸ τοῦ Ὑπίου
στάδιοι ἑκατόν, καὶ ἀπὸ τοῦ Λιλαίου εἰς Ἔλαιον
ἑξήκοντα. ἐνθένδε εἰς Κάλητα, ἄλλο ἐμπόριον, εἴκοσι
iii καὶ ἑκατόν. ἀπὸ Κάλητος εἰς Λύκον ποταμὸν
ὀγδοήκοντα, ἀπὸ δὲ Λύκου εἰς Ἡράκλειαν πόλιν

– was pointed out, where, legend has it, Prometheus was strung up by Hephaistos, as instructed by Zeus.

12 The coast from the Thracian Bosporus as far as
ii   Trapezous is like this. The Sanctuary of Zeus Ourios is 120 stades from Byzantium, and it is here that the narrows, called the mouth of the Pontus, enter the Propontis. These things that I tell you, you
iii already know. But on sailing from the Sanctuary to the right, there is the river Rhebas; it is 90 stades from the Sanctuary of Zeus. Thereafter, the Black Cape, as it is called, is 150 stades away. From the Black Cape to the river Artane, where there is a mooring for small vessels near the Sanctuary of
iv Aphrodite, it is another 150. From the Artane to the river Psilis it is 150; small boats can be moored near the rock that emerges not far from the mouth of the river. From there to Kalpes Limen it is 210
v   stades. Of Kalpes Limen, of the nature of the place and of its mooring, of the spring there of cold, pure water, and of the forest, infested with wild beasts, of shipbuilding wood near the sea, Xenophon the Elder spoke.

13   Kalpes Limen to Rhoe is 20 stades; there is a mooring for small ships there. From Rhoe to the small island of Apollonia, a short distance from the mainland, is another 20. There is a harbour at the bottom of the island. From there to Chelai is also 20 stades. 180 from Chelai is where the river Sangarios
ii   flows into the Euxine. From there to the mouth of the Hypios is another 180. To the *emporium* of Lilaion from the Hypios is 100 stades, and from

Ἑλληνίδα Δωρικήν, Μεγαρέων ἄποικον, στάδιοι
εἴκοσιν. ἐν Ἡρακλείᾳ ὅρμος ναυσίν. ἀπὸ δὲ
Ἡρακλείας ἐπὶ μὲν τὸ Μητρῷον καλούμενον στάδιοι
iv ὀγδοήκοντα. ἐνθένδε εἰς τὸ Ποσείδειον τετταράκοντα,
καὶ ἔνθεν εἰς Τυνδαρίδας πέντε καὶ τετταράκοντα,
πέντε δὲ καὶ δέκα ἔνθεν ἐπὶ τὸ Νυμφαῖον. καὶ ἀπὸ τοῦ
Νυμφαίου ἐπὶ τὸν Ὀξίναν ποταμὸν τριάκοντα. καὶ
v ἀπ᾽ Ὀξίνου εἰς Σανδαράκην ἐνενήκοντα. Σανδαράκη
ὅρμος ναυσὶ σμικραῖς. ἐνθένδε εἰς Κρηνίδας
ἑξήκοντα. καὶ ἀπὸ Κρηνίδων εἰς Ψύλλαν ἐμπόριον
τριάκοντα. ἐνθένδε εἰς Τίον, πόλιν Ἑλληνίδα
Ἰωνικήν, ἐπὶ θαλάττῃ οἰκουμένην, Μιλησίων καὶ
ταύτην ἄποικον, ἐνενήκοντα. ἀπὸ δὲ Τίου εἰς
Βιλλαῖον ποταμὸν στάδιοι εἴκοσιν. ἀπὸ δὲ Βιλλαίου
ἐπὶ τὸν Παρθένιον ποταμὸν στάδιοι ἑκατόν. μέχρι
τοῦδε Θρᾷκες οἱ Βιθυνοὶ νέμονται, ὧν καὶ Ξενοφῶν
ἐν τῇ συγγραφῇ μνήμην ἐποιήσατο ὅτι μαχιμώτατοι
εἶεν τῶν κατὰ τὴν Ἀσίαν, καὶ τὰ πολλὰ κακὰ ἡ
στρατιὰ τῶν Ἑλλήνων ὅτι ἐν τῇδε τῇ χώρᾳ ἔπαθεν,
ἐπειδὴ ἀπεχωρίσθησαν οἱ Ἀρκάδες ἀπό τε τῆς
Χειρισόφου καὶ τῆς Ξενοφῶντος μερίδος.

14 Τὰ δὲ ἀπὸ τοῦδε ἤδη Παφλαγονία. ἀπὸ Παρθενίου
εἰς Ἄμαστριν πόλιν Ἑλληνίδα στάδιοι ἐνενήκοντα ·
ὅρμος ναυσίν. ἔνθεν εἰς Ἐρυθίνους ἑξήκοντα. καὶ ἀπ᾽
ii Ἐρυθίνων εἰς Κρῶμναν ἄλλοι ἑξήκοντα. ἐνθένδε εἰς
Κύτωρον ἐνενήκοντα · ὅρμος ναυσὶν ἐν Κυτώρῳ. καὶ
ἀπὸ Κυτώρου εἰς Αἰγιαλοὺς ἑξήκοντα. εἰς δὲ Θύμηνα
iii ἐνενήκοντα. καὶ εἰς Κάραμβιν εἴκοσι καὶ ἑκατόν.
ἐνθένδε εἰς Ζεφύριον ἑξήκοντα. ἀπὸ δὲ Ζεφυρίου εἰς
Ἀβώνου τεῖχος, πόλιν σμικράν, πεντήκοντα καὶ
ἑκατόν. ὅρμος ναυσὶν οὐκ ἀσφαλής · σαλεύοιεν δ᾽ ἂν
ἀπαθεῖς, εἰ μὴ μέγας χειμὼν κατέχοι. ἀπὸ δὲ

Lilaion to Elaion is 60. From there to Kales,
iii another *emporium*, is 120. From Kales to the river
Lykos is 80, and from the Lykos to the Doric Greek
city of Herakleia, a colony of the Megarians, is 100
stades. In Herakleia there is mooring for ships.
From Herakleia to the so-called Metroön is 80
iv stades. From there to Posideion is 40, and from
there to Tyndaridai 45, and 15 from there to
Nymphaion. From Nymphaion to the river Oxinas is
30. And from the Oxinas to Sandarake, 90.
v Sandarake has a mooring for small ships. From
there to Krenidai, 60. From Krenidai to the
emporium Psylla, 30. From there to Tios, an Ionian
Greek city, built on the sea, and a colony of the
Milesians, 90. From Tios to the river Billaios is 20
stades. From Billaios to the river Parthenios is 100
stades. Up to here live Bithynian Thracians, of
whom Xenophon also made mention in his writings,
to the effect that they were the most bellicose
people in Asia, and that it was in their territory
that the Greek army suffered most of their
hardships after the Arcadians had been separated
from the portion of Cheirisophos and Xenophon.
14 From here onwards is Paphlagonia. From the
Parthenios to the Greek city of Amastris is 90
stades; a mooring for ships. From there to
Erythinoi, 60. And from Erythinoi to Kromna,
ii another 60. From there to Kytoros, 90; there is a
mooring for ships in Kytoros. And from Kytoros to
iii Aigialoi, 60. To Thymena, 90. And to Karambis,
120. From there to Zephyrion, 60. From
Zephyrion to Abonouteichos, a little town, 150.

Ἀβώνου τείχους εἰς Αἰγινήτην ἄλλοι πεντήκοντα καὶ
ἑκατόν. ἐνθένδε εἰς Κίνωλιν ἐμπόριον ἄλλοι
ἑξήκοντα · καὶ ἐν Κινώλει σαλεύοιεν ἂν νῆες ὥρᾳ
iv ἔτους. ἀπὸ δὲ Κινώλιος εἰς Στεφάνην ὀγδοήκοντα
καὶ ἑκατόν · ὅρμος ναυσὶν ἀσφαλής. ἀπὸ δὲ
Στεφάνης εἰς Ποταμοὺς πεντήκοντα καὶ ἑκατόν.
ἐνθένδε εἰς Λεπτὴν ἄκραν ἑκατὸν καὶ εἴκοσιν. ἀπὸ δὲ
Λεπτῆς ἄκρας εἰς Ἀρμένην ἑξήκοντα · λιμὴν αὐτόθι.
v καὶ Ξενοφῶν τῆς Ἀρμένης ἐμνημόνευσεν. καὶ ἔνθεν
εἰς Σινώπην στάδιοι τετταράκοντα · Σινωπεῖς
Μιλησίων ἄποικοι. ἀπὸ δὲ Σινώπης εἰς Κάρουσαν
πεντήκοντα καὶ ἑκατόν · σάλος ναυσίν. ἐνθένδε εἰς
Ζάγωρα ἄλλοι αὖ πεντήκοντα καὶ ἑκατόν · ἐνθένδε
εἰς τὸν Ἅλυν ποταμὸν τριακόσιοι.
15 Οὗτος ὁ ποταμὸς πάλαι μὲν ὅρος ἦν τῆς Κροίσου
βασιλείας καὶ τῆς Περσῶν, νῦν δὲ ὑπὸ τῇ Ῥωμαίων
ἐπικρατείᾳ ῥέει, οὐκ ἀπὸ μεσημβρίας, ὡς λέγει
Ἡρόδοτος, ἀλλ᾽ ἀπὸ ἀνίσχοντος ἡλίου. καθ᾽ ὅ τι δὲ
ii εἰσβάλλει εἰς τὸν Πόντον, ὁρίζει τὰ Σινωπέων καὶ
Ἀμισηνῶν ἔργα. ἀπὸ δὲ Ἅλυος ποταμοῦ εἰς
Ναύσταθμον στάδιοι ἐνενήκοντα, ἵναπερ καὶ λίμνη
ἐστίν. ἐνθένδε εἰς Κωνωπεῖον ἄλλην λίμνην ἄλλοι αὖ
πεντήκοντα. ἀπὸ δὲ Κωνωπείου εἰς Εὐσήνην ἑκατὸν
iii καὶ εἴκοσιν. ἐνθένδε εἰς Ἀμισὸν ἑκατὸν καὶ ἑξήκοντα.
Ἀμισός, πόλις Ἑλληνίς, Ἀθηναίων ἄποικος, ἐπὶ
θαλάττῃ οἰκεῖται. ἀπὸ δὲ Ἀμισοῦ εἰς Ἀγκῶνα
λιμένα, ἵναπερ καὶ ὁ Ἶρις εἰσβάλλει εἰς τὸν Πόντον,
στάδιοι ἑξήκοντα καὶ ἑκατόν. ἀπὸ δὲ τοῦ Ἴριος τῶν
ἐκβολῶν εἰς Ἡράκλειον ἑξήκοντα καὶ τριακόσιοι ·
ὅρμος ναυσίν. ἐνθένδε ἐπὶ τὸν Θερμώδοντα ποταμὸν
τετταράκοντα. οὗτος ὁ Θερμώδων ἐστίν, ἵναπερ αἱ
Ἀμαζόνες οἰκῆσαι λέγονται.

The mooring is not secure for ships; though they can ride at anchor without harm, unless a large storm blows up. From Abonouteichos to Aiginetes, another 150. From there to the *emporium* Kinolis, another 60; and at Kinolis ships may ride at anchor during
iv the summer. From Kinolis to Stephane, 180; there is a safe mooring for ships. From Stephane to Potamoi, 150. From there to Lepte Point, 120. From Lepte Point to Armene, 60; there is a harbour. Xenophon
v also mentions Armene. And from there to Sinope is 40 stades; the Sinopeans are colonists of the Milesians. From Sinope to Karousa, 150; there is an anchorage for ships. From there to Zagora is again another 150; from there to the river Halys is 30.

15 This river was of old the boundary between the kingdoms of Croesus and of the Persians, and now flows under Roman rule – not from the south, as Herodotus says, but from the direction of the rising sun. And there, where it flows into the Euxine, it separates the territories of the
ii Sinopeans and the Amisenians. From the river Halys to Naustathmos, where there is a harbour, is 90 stades. From there to Konopeion, another harbour, again 50. From Konopeion to Eusene,
iii 120. From there to Amisos, 160. Amisos, a Greek city, and a colony of the Athenians, is built on the sea. From Amisos to the harbour at Ankon, where the Iris flows out into the Euxine, is 160 stades. From the mouth of the Iris to Herakleion, 360; a mooring for ships. From there to the river Thermodon, 40. This Thermodon is where, they say, the Amazons lived.

16 Ἀπὸ δὲ Θερμώδοντος εἰς Βῆριν ποταμὸν στάδιοι
ἐνενήκοντα. ἐνθένδε εἰς Θόαριν ποταμὸν ἑξήκοντα.
ἀπὸ δὲ Θοάριος εἰς Οἰνόην τριάκοντα. ἀπ᾽ Οἰνόης εἰς
Φιγαμοῦντα ποταμὸν τετταράκοντα. ἐνθένδε εἰς

ii Φαδισάνην φρούριον πεντήκοντα καὶ ἑκατόν. ἐνθένδε
εἰς Πολεμώνιον πόλιν στάδιοι δέκα. ἀπὸ Πολεμωνίου
εἰς ἄκραν Ἰασόνιον καλουμένην στάδιοι τριάκοντα
καὶ ἑκατόν. ἐνθένδε εἰς Κιλίκων νῆσον πεντεκαίδεκα

iii στάδιοι. ἀπὸ δὲ Κιλίκων νήσου εἰς Βοῶνα πέντε καὶ
ἑβδομήκοντα. ἐν Βοῶνι ὅρμος ναυσίν. ἐνθένδε εἰς
Κοτύωρα ἐνενήκοντα. ταύτης ὡς πόλεως Ξενοφῶν
ἐμνεμόνευσεν, καὶ λέγει Σινωπέων ἄποικον εἶναι · νῦν
δὲ κώμη ἐστίν, καὶ οὐδὲ αὐτὴ μεγάλη. ἀπὸ
Κοτυώρων εἰς Μελάνθιον ποταμὸν στάδιοι μάλιστα
ἑξήκοντα. ἐνθένδε εἰς Φαρματηνὸν ἄλλον ποταμὸν
πεντήκοντα καὶ ἑκατόν. καὶ ἔνθεν εἰς Φαρνακείαν

iv εἴκοσι καὶ ἑκατόν. αὕτη ἡ Φαρνακεία πάλαι
Κερασοῦς ἐκαλεῖτο, Σινωπέων καὶ αὕτη ἄποικος.
ἐνθένδε εἰς τὴν Ἀρητιάδα νῆσον τριάκοντα. καὶ ἔνθεν
εἰς Ζεφύριον εἴκοσι καὶ ἑκατόν · ὅρμος ναυσίν. ἀπὸ
δὲ Ζεφυρίου εἰς Τρίπολιν στάδιοι ἐνενήκοντα. ἐνθένδε

v εἰς τὰ Ἀργύρια στάδιοι εἴκοσιν. ἐκ δὲ τῶν Ἀργυρίων
εἰς Φιλοκάλειαν ἐνενήκοντα. ἐνθένδε εἰς Κόραλλα
ἑκατόν. ἀπὸ δὲ Κοράλλων εἰς Ἱερὸν ὄρος πεντήκοντα
καὶ ἑκατόν. ἀπὸ δὲ Ἱεροῦ ὄρους εἰς Κορδύλην

vi τετταράκοντα · ὅρμος ναυσίν. ἀπὸ δὲ Κορδύλης εἰς
Ἑρμώνασσαν πέντε καὶ τετταράκοντα · καὶ δεῦρο
ὅρμος. ἀπὸ δὲ Ἑρμωνάσσης εἰς Τραπεζοῦντα στάδιοι
ἑξήκοντα. ἐνταῦθα σὺ ποιεῖς λιμένα · πάλαι γάρ,
ὅσον ἀποσαλεύειν ὥρᾳ ἔτους, ὅρμος ἦν.

17 Τὰ δὲ ἀπὸ Τραπεζοῦντος διαστήματα μέχρι
Διοσκουριάδος προείρηται διὰ τῶν ποταμῶν

16 From the Thermodon to the river Beris is 90 stades. From there to the river Thoaris, 60. From the Thoaris to Oinoe, 30. From Oinoe to the river Phigamous, 40. From there to the fort at
ii Phadisane, 150. From there to the city of Polemonion is 10 stades. From Polemonion to the so-called Jason's Point is 130 stades. From there
iii to the island of the Cilicians is 15 stades. From the island of the Cilicians to Boön, 75. In Boön there is a mooring for ships. From there to Kotyora, 90. Xenophon mentioned this town, and said that it was a colony of the Sinopeans; now it is a village, and not a large one. From Kotyora to the river Melanthios is about 60 stades. From there to
iv the Pharmatenos, another river, 150. And from there to Pharnakeia, 120. This Pharnakeia used to be called Kerasous, and was a colony of the Sinopeans. From there to the island of Aretias, 30. From there to Zephyrion, 120; there is a mooring for ships. From Zephyrion to Tripolis is 90 stades. From there to the Argyria is 20 stades.
v From the Argyria to Philokaleia, 90. From there to Koralla, 100. From Koralla to the Sacred Mount, 150. From the Sacred Mount to Kordyle,
v 40; there is a mooring for ships. From Kordyle to Hermonassa, 45. Here too is a mooring. From Hermonassa to Trapezous is 60 stades. There you are building a harbour; for before, there was a mooring where one could only ride at anchor in the summer.

17 The intervals between Trapezous as far as Dioskourias are already given by the measurements

ἀναμετρηθέντα. ἀθροίζονται δὲ ἀπὸ Τραπεζοῦντος εἰς Διοσκουριάδα, τὴν νῦν Σεβαστόπολιν καλουμένην, στάδιοι δισχίλιοι διακόσιοι ἑξήκοντα.

ii Τάδε μὲν [οὖν] τὰ ἀπὸ Βυζαντίου πλεόντων ἐν δεξιᾷ ὡς ἐπὶ Διοσκουριάδα, εἰς ὅπερ στρατόπεδον τελευτᾷ Ῥωμαίοις ἡ ἐπικράτεια ἐν δεξιᾷ εἰσπλεόντων iii εἰς τὸν Πόντον. ἐπεὶ δὲ ἐπυθόμην Κότυν τετελευτηκέναι, τὸν βασιλέα τοῦ Βοσπόρου τοῦ Κιμμερίου καλουμένου, ἐπιμελὲς ἐποιησάμην καὶ τὸν μέχρι τοῦ Βοσπόρου πλοῦν δηλῶσαί σοι · ὡς, εἴ τι βουλεύοιο περὶ τοῦ Βοσπόρου, ὑπάρχοι σοι καὶ τόνδε τὸν πλοῦν μὴ ἀγνοοῦντι βουλεύεσθαι.

18 Ὁρμηθεῖσιν οὖν ἐκ Διοσκουριάδος, πρῶτος ἂν εἴη ὅρμος ἐν Πιτυοῦντι · στάδιοι τριακόσιοι πεντήκοντα. ἐνθένδε εἰς τὴν Νιτικὴν στάδιοι πεντήκοντα καὶ ἑκατόν, ἵναπερ πάλαι ᾤκει ἔθνος Σκυθικόν, οὗ ii μνήμην ποιεῖται ὁ λογοποιὸς Ἡρόδοτος. καὶ λέγει τούτους εἶναι τοὺς φθειροτρωκτέοντας · καὶ γὰρ εἰς τοῦτο ἔτι ἡ δόξα ἡ αὐτὴ ὑπὲρ αὐτῶν κατέχει. ἐκ δὲ Νιτικῆς εἰς Ἄβασκον ποταμὸν στάδιοι ἐνενήκοντα. ὁ δὲ Βόργυς τοῦ Ἀβάσκου διέχει σταδίους ἑκατὸν καὶ εἴκοσιν, καὶ ὁ Νῆσις τοῦ Βόργυς, ἵναπερ καὶ iii Ἡράκλειον ἄκραν ἔχει, σταδίους ἑξήκοντα. ἀπὸ δὲ Νήσιος εἰς Μασαϊτικὴν στάδιοι ἐνενήκοντα. ἐνθένδε εἰς Ἀχαιοῦντα στάδιοι ἑξήκοντα, ὅσπερ ποταμὸς διορίζει Ζιλχοὺς καὶ Σανίγας. Ζιλχῶν βασιλεὺς Σταχέμφαξ · καὶ οὗτος παρὰ σοῦ τὴν βασιλείαν ἔσχεν. ἀπ᾽ Ἀχαιοῦντος εἰς Ἡράκλειαν ἄκραν πεντήκοντα καὶ ἑκατὸν στάδιοι. ἐνθένδε εἰς ἄκραν, ἵναπερ σκέπη ἐστὶν ἀνέμου θρασκίου καὶ βορρᾶ, iv ὀγδοήκοντα καὶ ἑκατόν. ἐνθένδε εἰς τὴν καλουμένην

between the rivers. They amount collectively from Trapezous to Dioskourias, now called Sebastopolis, to 2,260 stades.

ii   Thus, then, is the voyage sailing to the right from Byzantium to Dioskourias, the camp which is the limit of Roman control when one sails to the

iii right of the Euxine Sea. But when we heard that Kotys, king of the so-called Kimmerian Bosporus, had died, I decided that it was my duty to explain the voyage as far as the Bosporus to you, so that, if you were planning something with regard to the Bosporus, you would be able to plan it without being ignorant of the voyage.

18 Setting out from Dioskourias, then, the first mooring would be at Pityous; it is 350 stades. From there it is 150 stades to Nitike, where a Scythian tribe used to live of old, of whom the

ii   writer Herodotus makes mention. He says that they are all eaters of fir-cones; and still people hold that opinion concerning them. From Nitike to the river Abaskos is 90 stades. And the Borgys is 120 stades distant from the Abaskos, and the Nesis 60 from the Borgys, where Herakleion

iii Point is. From the Nesis to Masaïtike is 90 stades. From there to the Achaious is 60 stades, which river separates the Zilchoi and the Sanigai. King of the Zilchoi is Stachemphax; and he holds his kingdom from you. From the Achaious to Herakleia Point is 150 stades. From there to the point which is a shelter from the

iv   Thraskian and north winds, 180. From there to

Παλαιὰν Λαζικὴν εἴκοσι καὶ ἑκατὸν στάδιοι. ἐνθένδε
εἰς τὴν Παλαιὰν Ἀχαιῖαν πεντήκοντα καὶ ἑκατόν · καὶ
ἔνθεν εἰς Πάγρας λιμένα πεντήκοντα καὶ τριακόσιοι.
ἀπὸ δὲ Πάγρας λιμένος εἰς Ἱερὸν λιμένα ὀγδοήκοντα
καὶ ἑκατόν. ἐνθένδε εἰς Σινδικὴν τριακόσιοι.

19 Ἀπὸ δὲ Σινδικῆς εἰς Βόσπορον τὸν Κιμμέριον
καλούμενον καὶ πόλιν τοῦ Βοσπόρου Παντικάπαιον
τετταράκοντα καὶ πεντακόσιοι. ἐνθένδε ἐπὶ Τάναϊν
ποταμὸν ἑξήκοντα, ὃς λέγεται ὁρίζειν ἀπὸ τῆς Ἀσίας
τὴν Εὐρώπην. καὶ ὁρμᾶται μὲν ἀπὸ λίμνης τῆς
Μαιώτιδος, εἰσβάλλει δὲ εἰς θάλατταν τὴν τοῦ
ii Εὐξείνου Πόντου. καίτοι Αἰσχύλος ἐν Προμηθεῖ
Λυομένῳ τὸν Φᾶσιν ὅρον τῆς Εὐρώπης καὶ τῆς Ἀσίας
ποιεῖ. λέγουσι γοῦν [παρ'] αὐτῷ οἱ Τιτᾶνες πρὸς τὸν
Προμηθέα ὅτι

ἥκομεν
τοὺς σοὺς ἄθλους τούσδε, Προμηθεῦ,
δεσμοῦ τε πάθος τόδ' ἐποψόμενοι.

ἔπειτα καταλέγουσιν, ὅσην χώραν ἐπῆλθον ·

πῇ μὲν δίδουμον χθονὸς Εὐρώπης
μέγαν ἠδ' Ἀσίας τέρμονα Φᾶσιν.

iii Τῆς δὲ λίμνης τῆς Μαιώτιδος περίπλους ἐν κύκλῳ
λέγεται σταδίων ἀμφὶ τοὺς ἐνακισχιλίους. ἀπὸ δὲ
Παντικαπαίου εἰς κώμην Καζέκα ἐπὶ θαλάττῃ
ᾠκισμένην στάδιοι εἴκοσι καὶ τετρακόσιοι. ἐνθένδε
εἰς Θεοδοσίαν, πόλιν ἐρήμην, στάδιοι ὀγδοήκοντα καὶ
iv διακόσιοι. καὶ αὕτη πάλαι ἦν Ἑλλὰς πόλις, Ἰωνική,
Μιλησίων ἄποικος, καὶ μνήμη ἐστὶν αὐτῆς ἐν πολλοῖς
γράμμασιν. ἐνθένδε εἰς λιμένα Σκυθοταύρων ἔρημον
στάδιοι διακόσιοι · καὶ ἔνθεν εἰς Λαμπάδα τῆς

Palaia Lazike, as it is called, is 120 stades. From
there to Palaia Achaia, 150; and from there to
Pagra Limen, 350. From Pagra Limen to the
Sacred Harbour, 180. From there to Sindike,
300.

19 From Sindike to the so-called Kimmerian
Bosporus and the Bosporan city Pantikapaion,
540. From there to the river Tanaïs, which is said
to divide Europe from Asia, 60. And it starts
from the Maiotis lake, and flows into the sea at
ii the Euxine. Aeschylus, however, in *Prometheus
Unbound*, made the Phasis the boundary of
Europe and Asia. The Titans, at any rate, tell
Prometheus,

> We have come, Prometheus, to witness
> Your struggle, and your torment in chains.

Then they recount the lands they have come
through:

> Where the soils of Europe and Asia
> Have a common limit in the great Phasis.

iii It is said that the circumnavigation around the
Maiotis lake is about 9,000 stades. From
Pantikapaios to the village of Kazeka, which is
built on the sea, is 420 stades. From there to
iv Theodosia, a deserted city, is 280 stades. It used
to be an Ionian Greek city, a colony of the
Milesians, and there is a mention of it in many
works. From there to the deserted harbour of the
Skythotaurians is 200 stades; and from there to
v Tauric Lampas is 600 stades. From Lampas to

v Ταυρικῆς στάδιοι ἑξακόσιοι. ἀπὸ δὲ Λαμπάδος εἰς
Συμβόλου λιμένα, Ταυρικὸν καὶ τοῦτον, στάδιοι
εἴκοσι καὶ πεντακόσιοι. καὶ ἔνθεν εἰς Χερρόνησον τῆς
Ταυρικῆς ὀγδοήκοντα καὶ ἑκατόν. ἀπὸ δὲ
Χερρονήσου εἰς Κερκινῖτιν στάδιοι ἑξακόσιοι, καὶ
ἀπὸ Κερκινίτιδος εἰς Καλὸν λιμένα, Σκυθικὸν καὶ
τοῦτον, ἄλλοι ἑπτακόσιοι.

20 Ἐκ δὲ Καλοῦ λιμένος εἰς Ταμυράκην τριακόσιοι ·
ἔσω δὲ τῆς Ταμυράκης λίμνη ἐστὶν οὐ μεγάλη. καὶ
ἔνθεν εἰς τὰς ἐκροὰς τῆς λίμνης ἄλλοι τριακόσιοι. ἐκ
δὲ τῶν ἐκροῶν τῆς λίμνης εἰς Ἡϊόνας στάδιοι
ὀγδοήκοντα καὶ τριακόσιοι. καὶ ἔνθεν εἰς ποταμὸν
ii Βορυσθένην πεντήκοντα καὶ ἑκατόν. κατὰ δὲ τὸν
Βορυσθένην ἄνω πλέοντι πόλις Ἑλλὰς ὄνομα Ὀλβία
πεπόλισται. ἀπὸ δὲ Βορυσθένους ἐπὶ νῆσον σμικράν,
ἐρήμην καὶ ἀνώνυμον, στάδιοι ἑξήκοντα. καὶ ἔνθεν
εἰς Ὀδησσὸν ὀγδοήκοντα. ἐν Ὀδησσῷ ὅρμος ναυσίν.
ἀπὸ δὲ Ὀδησσοῦ ἔχεται Ἰστριανῶν λιμήν. στάδιοι εἰς
iii αὐτὸν πεντήκοντα καὶ διακόσιοι. ἐνθένδε ἔχεται
Ἰσιακῶν λιμήν. στάδιοι εἰς αὐτὸν πεντήκοντα. καὶ
ἔνθεν εἰς τὸ Ψιλὸν καλούμενον στόμα τοῦ Ἴστρου
διακόσιοι καὶ χίλιοι. τὰ δὲ ἐν μέσῳ ἔρημα καὶ
ἀνώνυμα.

21 Κατὰ τοῦτο μάλιστα τὸ στόμα ἐπ᾽ εὐθὺ πλέοντι
ἀνέμῳ ἀπαρκτίᾳ ἰδίως τὸ πέλαγος νῆσος πρόσκειται,
ἥντινα οἱ μὲν Ἀχιλλέως νῆσον, οἱ δὲ Δρόμον
Ἀχιλλέως, οἱ δὲ Λευκὴν ἐπὶ τῆς χροᾶς ὀνομάζουσιν.
ταύτην λέγεται Θέτις ἀνεῖναι τῷ παιδί, καὶ ταύτην
οἰκεῖν τὸν Ἀχιλλέα. καὶ νεώς ἐστιν ἐν αὐτῇ τοῦ
ii Ἀχιλλέως, καὶ ξόανον τῆς παλαιᾶς ἐργασίας. ἡ δὲ
νῆσος ἀνθρώπων μὲν ἐρήμη ἐστίν, νέμεται δὲ αἰξὶν οὐ
πολλαῖς. καὶ ταύτας ἀνατιθέναι λέγονται τῷ Ἀχιλλεῖ

Symbolos harbour, also in Tauris, is 520 stades. And from there to the Tauric Cherronesos, 180. From Cherronesos to Kerkinitis is 600 stades, and from Kerkinitis to Kalos Limen, also in Scythia, another 700.

20 From Kalos Limen to Tamyrake, 300; within Tamyrake there is a lake, which is not large. From there to the outflow of the lake, another 300. From the outflow of the lake to Eion is 380 stades. From there to the river Borysthenes, 150.

ii On the Borysthenes, upstream, a Greek city, called Olbia, has been built. From the Borysthenes to a small island, deserted and nameless, is 60 stades. And from there to Odessos, 80. In Odessos there is a mooring for ships. After Odessos comes the harbour of the

iii Istrians. It is 250 stades to there. After there comes the harbour of the Isiakoi. It is 150 stades to there. And from there to the mouth of the Ister called Psilon, 1,200. The stretch between is deserted and nameless.

21 Just about opposite this mouth – straight across the open sea, especially when you sail with the Aparktias wind – lies an island, which some call Achilles' Island, others Achilles' Racetrack, and others still Leuke, because of its colour. It is said that Thetis set it up for her son, and that Achilles lived there. And there is a temple of Achilles there, and a wooden statue of ancient workmanship.

ii The island is deserted of humans, but a few goats live there – they say that those who put in there dedicate one to Achilles – and there are many

ὅσοι προσίσχουσιν. καὶ ἄλλα πολλὰ ἀναθήματα
ἀνάκειται ἐν τῷ νεῷ, φιάλαι καὶ δακτύλιοι καὶ λίθοι
τῶν πολυτελεστέρων · ταῦτα ξύμπαντα χαριστήρια
τῷ Ἀχιλλεῖ ἀνάκειται, καὶ ἐπιγράμματα, τὰ μὲν
Ῥωμαϊκῶς τὰ δὲ Ἑλληνικῶς πεποιημένα ἐν ἄλλῳ καὶ
ἐν ἄλλῳ μέτρῳ, ἔπαινοι τοῦ Ἀχιλλέως, ἔστι δὲ ἃ καὶ
iii τοῦ Πατρόκλου · καὶ γὰρ καὶ τὸν Πάτροκλον τιμῶσιν
ξὺν τῷ Ἀχιλλεῖ ὅσοι τῷ Ἀχιλλεῖ χαρίζεσθαι
ἐθέλουσιν. ὄρνιθες δὲ πολλοὶ αὐλίζονται ἐν τῇ νήσῳ,
λάροι καὶ αἴθυιαι καὶ κορῶναι αἱ θαλάττιοι τὸ πλῆθος
iv οὐ σταθμητοί. οὗτοι οἱ ὄρνιθες θεραπεύουσι τοῦ
Ἀχιλλέως τὸν νεών. ἕωθεν ὁσημέραι καταπέτονται
εἰς τὴν θάλατταν · ἔπειτα ἀπὸ τῆς θαλάττης
βεβρεγμένοι τὰ πτερὰ σπουδῇ αὖ εἰσπέτονται εἰς τὸν
νεών, καὶ ῥαίνουσι τὸν νεών. ἐπειδὰν δὲ καλῶς ἔχῃ,
οἳ δὲ ἐκκαλλύνουσιν αὖ τὸ ἔδαφος τοῖς πτεροῖς.

22 Οἳ δὲ καὶ τάδε ἱστοροῦσιν · τῶν προσεσχηκότων τῇ
νήσῳ, ἱερεῖα τοὺς μὲν ἐξεπίτηδες πλέοντας εἰς αὐτὴν
ἐπὶ ταῖς ναυσὶν κομίζειν, καὶ τούτων τὰ μὲν καταθύειν,
ii τὰ δὲ ἀφιέναι τῷ Ἀχιλλεῖ · τοὺς δέ τινας ὑπὸ
χειμῶνος ἐξαναγκασθέντας προσέχειν, καὶ τούτους
παρ' αὐτοῦ τοῦ θεοῦ αἰτεῖν ἱερεῖον, χρωμένους ἐπὶ
τῶν ἱερείων εἰ λῷόν σφισιν καὶ ἄμεινον θῦσαι ὅ τι περ
αὐτοὶ τῇ γνώμῃ ἐπιλέξαιντο νεμόμενον, τιμὴν ἅμα
iii καταβάλλοντες τὴν ἀξίαν σφίσιν δοκοῦσαν. εἰ δὲ
ἀπαγορεύοι ὁ χρησμός — εἶναι γὰρ χρησμοὺς ἐν τῷ
νεῷ — προσβάλλειν τῇ τιμῇ · εἰ δὲ ἔτι ἀπαγορεύοι, ἔτι
προσβάλλειν · συγχωρήσαντος δέ, γιγνώσκειν ὅτι
iv ἀποχρῶσα ἡ τιμή ἐστιν. τὸ δὲ ἱερεῖον ἵστασθαι ἐπὶ
τῷδε αὐτόματον, μηδὲ ἀποφεύγειν ἔτι. καὶ τοῦτο δὴ
πολὺ ἀνακεῖσθαι τὸ ἀργύριον τῷ ἥρῳ τὰς τιμὰς τῶν
ἱερείων.

other votive offerings set up in the temple – bowls
and rings and very costly stones. All these thank-
offerings are laid up for Achilles, as well as
inscriptions, some in Latin, some in Greek, in
iii various meters, praising Achilles; and there are
some for Patroclus too, for those who wish to pray
to Achilles also honour Patroclus along with him.
Many birds also live on the island – cormorants,
gulls, and sea-crows in an innumerable quantity.
iv These birds attend to the temple of Achilles.
Each morning they fly down to the sea; then,
having wetted their wings in the sea, they quickly
fly up again to the temple, and sprinkle it. When
this has been done thoroughly, they wash the
pavement, again with their wings.

22 There are also those who say this: that of those
who put in to the island, the ones who have
deliberately sailed there bring offerings on board
their ships, and sacrifice one part of them, leaving
ii the other free for Achilles; whereas others are
forced to land by a storm, and ask for a victim
from the god himself, whom they consult
regarding the sacrifices – whether it is better and
preferable for them to sacrifice whatever animal
they have taken, according to their liking, from
the pasture – while depositing the sum which
iii seems appropriate to them. And if the oracle –
for there is an oracle in the temple – should refuse,
they add to that sum; if it should still refuse, still
they add; and when it agrees, they know that that
iv sum is sufficient. The victim then stands there of
its own accord, and no longer tries to escape. And

23 Φαίνεσθαι δὲ ἐνύπνιον τὸν Ἀχιλλέα τοῖς μὲν προσχοῦσι τῇ νήσῳ, τοῖς δὲ καὶ πλέουσιν, ἐπειδὰν οὐ πόρρω αὐτῆς ἀπόσχωσιν, καὶ φράζειν ὅπου προσχεῖν τῆς νήσου ἄμεινον καὶ ὅπου ὁρμίσασθαι. οἳ δὲ καὶ ὕπαρ λέγουσι φανῆναί σφισιν ἐπὶ τοῦ ἱστοῦ ἢ ἐπ' ἄκρου τοῦ κέρως τὸν Ἀχιλλέα, καθάπερ τοὺς

ii Διοσκόρους· τοσόνδε μόνον τῶν Διοσκούρων μεῖον ἔχειν τὸν Ἀχιλλέα, ὅσον οἱ μὲν Διόσκουροι τοῖς πανταχοῦ πλωϊζομένοις ἐναργεῖς φαίνονται, καὶ φανέντες σωτῆρες γίνονται, ὃ δὲ τοῖς πελάζουσιν ἤδη τῇ νήσῳ. οἳ δὲ καὶ τὸν Πάτροκλόν σφισιν ὀφθῆναι

iii ἐνύπνιον λέγουσιν. τάδε μὲν ὑπὲρ τῆς νήσου τῆς τοῦ Ἀχιλλέως ἀκοὴν ἀνέγραψα τῶν ἢ αὐτῶν προσχόντων, ἢ ἄλλων πεπυσμένων· καί μοι δοκεῖ οὐκ ἄπιστα

iv εἶναι. Ἀχιλλέα γὰρ ἐγὼ πείθομαι εἴπερ τινὰ καὶ ἄλλον ἥρωα εἶναι, τῇ τε εὐγενείᾳ τεκμαιρόμενος καὶ τῷ κάλλει καὶ τῇ ῥώμῃ τῆς ψυχῆς καὶ τῷ νέον μεταλλάξαι ἐξ ἀνθρώπων καὶ τῇ Ὁμήρου ἐπ' αὐτῷ ποιήσει καὶ τῷ ἐρωτικὸν γενέσθαι καὶ φιλέταιρον, ὡς καὶ ἐπαποθανεῖν ἑλέσθαι τοῖς παιδικοῖς.

24 Ἀπὸ δὲ τοῦ Ψιλοῦ καλουμένου στόματος τοῦ Ἴστρου εἰς τὸ δεύτερον στόμα στάδιοι ἑξήκοντα. ἐνθένδε ἐπὶ τὸ Καλὸν καλούμενον στόμα στάδιοι τετταράκοντα. καὶ ἀπὸ τοῦ Καλοῦ ἐπὶ τὸ Νάρακον ὧδε ὀνομαζόμενον στόμα τέταρτον τοῦ Ἴστρου στάδιοι

ii ἑξήκοντα. ἐνθένδε ἐπὶ τὸ πέμπτον εἴκοσι καὶ ἑκατόν· καὶ ἔνθεν εἰς Ἰστρίαν πόλιν στάδιοι πεντακόσιοι.

iii ἐνθένδε εἰς Τομέα πόλιν στάδιοι τριακόσιοι. ἀπὸ δὲ Τομέως εἰς Κάλλατιν πόλιν ἄλλοι τριακόσιοι· ὅρμος ναυσίν. ἐνθένδε εἰς Καρῶν λιμένα ὀγδοήκοντα καὶ ἑκατόν· καὶ ἡ γῆ ἐν κύκλῳ τοῦ λιμένος Καρία κληΐζεται. ἀπὸ δὲ Καρῶν λιμένος εἰς Τετρισιάδα

this is why there is so much money laid up to the hero as payment for the victims.

23 It is also said that Achilles appears in dreams to those who put in to the island, and to those who sail by when they are not far from it, and shows them where the best place on the island to put in is, and where to moor. And others say that Achilles has appeared to them when awake, on their sail or on the tip of the prow, like the

ii Dioskouroi; they say that Achilles is only inferior to the Dioskouroi in that the Dioskouroi appear visibly to sailors everywhere, and as saviours, whereas Achilles appears only to those already approaching the island. They also say that they

iii see Patroclus in dreams. These things that I have recorded about Achilles' Island are reports from those who have either landed there, or have learned it from others, and they do not seem

iv incredible to me. For I myself believe that Achilles was a hero second-to-none, for his nobility, beauty, and strength of soul; for his early departure from mankind, and for Homer's poem to him; and for the love and friendship because of which he wanted to die after his beloved.

24 From the mouth of the Ister called Psilon to the second mouth is 60 stades. From there to the mouth called Kalon is 40 stades, and from Kalon to Narakon, as the fourth mouth of the Ister is called,

ii is 60 stades. From there to the fifth, 120; and from there to the city of Istria, 500 stades. From there

iii to the city of Tomis is 300 stades. From Tomis to the city of Kallatis is another 300; there is a

στάδιοι εἴκοσι καὶ ἑκατόν. ἐνθένδε εἰς Βιζώνην,
iv χῶρον ἔρημον, στάδιοι ἑξήκοντα. ἀπὸ δὲ Βιζώνης εἰς
Διονυσόπολιν στάδιοι ὀγδοήκοντα. ἐνθένδε εἰς
Ὀδησσὸν διακόσιοι · ὅρμος ναυσίν. ἐκ δὲ Ὀδησσοῦ
εἰς τοῦ Αἵμου τὰς ὑπωρείας, αἲ δὴ εἰς τὸν Πόντον
καθήκουσιν, στάδιοι τριακόσιοι ἑξήκοντα · καὶ δεῦρο
v ὅρμος ναυσίν. ἐκ δὲ τοῦ Αἵμου εἰς Μεσημβρίαν πόλιν
ἐνενήκοντα · ὅρμος ναυσίν. καὶ ἐκ Μεσημβρίας εἰς
Ἀγχίαλον πόλιν στάδιοι ἑβδομήκοντα, καὶ ἐξ
Ἀγχιάλου εἰς Ἀπολλωνίαν ὀγδοήκοντα καὶ ἑκατόν.
vi αὗται πᾶσαι αἱ πόλεις Ἑλληνίδες εἰσίν, ᾠκισμέναι ἐν
τῇ Σκυθίᾳ, ἐν ἀριστερᾷ εἰσπλέοντι εἰς τὸν Πόντον.
ἐκ δὲ Ἀπολλωνίας εἰς Χερρόνησον στάδιοι ἑξήκοντα ·
ὅρμος ναυσίν. καὶ ἐκ Χερρονήσου εἰς Αὐλαίου τεῖχος
πεντήκοντα καὶ διακόσιοι. ἐνθένδε εἰς Θυνιάδα ἀκτὴν
εἴκοσι καὶ ἑκατόν.
25 Ἀπὸ δὲ Θυνιάδος εἰς Σαλμυδησσὸν στάδιοι
διακόσιοι. τούτου τοῦ χωρίου μνήμην πεποίηται
Ξενοφῶν ὁ πρεσβύτερος, καὶ μέχρι τούτου λέγει τὴν
στρατιὰν ἐλθεῖν τῶν Ἑλλήνων, ἧς αὐτὸς ἡγήσατο, ὅτε
ii τὰ τελευταῖα σὺν Σεύθῃ τῷ Θρᾳκὶ ἐστράτευσεν. καὶ
περὶ τῆς ἀλιμενότητος τοῦ χωρίου πολλὰ ἀνέγραψεν,
ὅτι ἐνταῦθα ἐκπίπτει τὰ πλοῖα χειμῶνι βιαζόμενα,
καὶ οἱ Θρᾷκες οἱ πρόσχωροι ὅτι ὑπὲρ τῶν ναυαγίων
iii ἐν σφίσιν διαμάχονται. ἀπὸ δὲ Σαλμυδησσοῦ εἰς
Φρυγίαν στάδιοι τριάκοντα καὶ τριακόσιοι. ἐνθένδε
ἐπὶ Κυανέας εἴκοσι καὶ τριακόσιοι. αὗται δὲ αἱ
Κυάνεαί εἰσιν, ἃς λέγουσιν οἱ ποιηταὶ πλαγκτὰς
πάλαι εἶναι, καὶ διὰ τούτων πρώτην ναῦν περᾶσαι τὴν
iv Ἀργώ, ἥτις εἰς Κόλχους Ἰάσονα ἤγαγεν. ἐκ δὲ
Κυανέων ἐπὶ τὸ Ἱερὸν τοῦ Διὸς τοῦ Οὐρίου, ἵναπερ τὸ
στόμα τοῦ Πόντου, στάδιοι τετταράκοντα. ἐνθένδε

mooring for ships. From there to the harbour of
the Karians, 180; and the land in a circle around
the harbour is called Karia. From the harbour of
the Karians to Tetrisias is 120 stades. From there
iv to Bizone, a deserted spot, is 60 stades. From
Bizone to Dionysopolis is 80 stades. From there to
Odessos is 200; there is a mooring for ships. From
Odessos to the foothills of Haimos, which falls
right down to the Sea, is 360 stades; and here there
v is a mooring for ships. From Haimos to the city of
Mesembria, 90; there is a mooring for ships. And
from Mesembria to the city of Anchialos is 70 stades;
vi and from Anchialos to Apollonia, 180. All these
are Greek cities, founded in Scythia, on the left-
hand side of one sailing into the Pontus. From
Apollonia to Cherronesos is 60 stades; there is a
mooring for ships. And from Cherronesos to
Aulaiouteichos, 250. From there to Thynias Point, 120.
25 From Thynias to Salmydessos is 200 stades.
Xenophon the Elder makes mention of this place:
it was to here, he says, that the Greek army came,
when he was its leader, when he campaigned for
ii the last time against Seuthes the Thracian. And
he wrote much concerning the place's lack of
harbours, the fleet's shipwreck when forced by a
storm, and the Thracians' fighting with him over
iii the wreckage. From Salmydessos to Phrygia is
330 stades. From there to the Kyaneai, 320.
These Kyaneai are those that the poets say once
used to wander, and through which the first ship,
the Argo, passed when it was carrying Jason to
iv Colchis. From the Kyaneai to the Sanctuary of

εἰς λιμένα Δάφνης τῆς Μαινομένης καλουμένης στάδιοι τετταράκοντα. ἀπὸ δὲ Δάφνης εἰς Βυζάντιον ὀγδοήκοντα.

τάδε μὲν καὶ τὰ ἀπὸ τοῦ Βοσπόρου τοῦ Κιμμερίου ἐπὶ Βόσπορον τὸν Θρᾴκιον καὶ πόλιν Βυζάντιον.

Zeus Ourios, which is at the mouth of the Sea, is 40 stades. From there to the harbour of Daphne, called the Insane, is 40 stades. From Daphne to Byzantium, 80.

These, then, are the things from the Kimmerian Bosporus to Thrace and the city of Byzantium.

Commentary

Note: figures in square brackets following place-names indicate map references in the *Barrington Atlas of the Greek and Roman World* (Princeton, 2000).

1-11. The first section of the Periplus *starts at Trapezous, and describes the voyage of inspection taken by Arrian as far as Sebastopolis, the limit of Roman military control over the eastern Black Sea coast.*

1 §1. *We came to Trapezous* .... Immediately Arrian sets the tone of the work, relating his journey to those of Hadrian and of Xenophon (for which see Xenophon, *Anabasis* IV.8.22f.), and using the second person to refer to the Emperor. Note Arrian's use of ἐκεῖνος, denoting something like '*the* Xenophon', 'that famous Xenophon', to differentiate himself from Xenophon; see Introduction, p.16. Arrian's insistence that it was 'the very same spot' as his two illustrious pathfinders from which he gazed down at the sea places all three men in a very definite historical continuum, emphasising the direct roots of Hadrian's new imperial culture in that of classical Greece.

Trapezous [87E4], now the Turkish city of Trabzon, was at various stages in its history one of the most important centres of the area. Founded in the eighth century BC as a colony of the Sinopeans, possibly as an *emporium* for the mineral wealth of the interior (for which see Drews [1976]), it became a Roman 'free city' after it sided with

Pompey against Mithridates in 64 BC. The city reached the zenith of its military importance following the conquest of Armenia and the construction of the Cappadocian *limes*, at the head of which it stood.

The port of Trapezous had been the base for the fleets of the independent kings of the region before the Roman conquest, and was taken over as such by the new régime. By Nero's reign, the port had taken on some importance by virtue of its strategic position; Corbulo's campaign against the Parthians was waged from there, and the fleet based there played a part in the wars of AD 69 (see Tacitus, *Hist.* III.47). It then turns up on the early third-century Dura-Europos shield, inscribed with the names of military stations on the Black Sea. See further Bryer and Winfield (1985), pp.178-80, Reddé (1986), pp.259-60, and note to 16.6 below for the harbour itself.

§2-4. *The altars* .... Arrian now reports on progress on construction of a sanctuary dedicated to Hadrian (and possibly to Rome as well), evidently in an imposing and landscape-dominating spot overlooking the sea. It may well have commemorated a visit by the Emperor, who inspected the Cappadocian frontier in 123/4 or 129, and whose habit of beautifying and improving the cities he visited is well-known (see Introduction, p.18; see also 16.6 for the new harbour which will have resulted from the same visit). See also note to 2.1-2 below for possible traces of this structure.

2 §1-2. Hadrian's visit also resulted, it seems, in a temple to Hermes and one Philesios, probably a local hero or the legendary founder of the city; and the description of the double cult mirrors nicely the similar arrangement at Leuke Island with Achilles and Patroclus (for which see 21 below).

Although no trace of the sanctuary or the temple buildings remains at Trapezous, the church of Chrysokephalos (or Fatih Camii), founded by

Constantine's nephew Hannibalianus at the northern end of the great spur of rock overlooking the sea that formed the ancient acropolis, incorporates a huge marble block bearing traces of a Greek inscription (mostly obliterated by a later Arabic one) dedicated to Hadrian, which probably belonged to one or other of these structures (Mitford [1974], 160-3). The size of the block makes it unlikely to have been moved very far from its original site, and the church was probably built on a former civic pagan site in the centre of the city, which perhaps makes the altar to Hadrian and Rome the more likely candidate.

§3. *Like Xenophon in Kalpes Limen ....* Arrian refers to *Anab.* VI.4.22.

3 §1. *Hyssou Limen* [87F4]. The ancient anchorage is the modern Araklıçarşısı (also known as Sürmene), at the mouth of the Kara Dere river. The fort has been located by Bryer and Winfield (1985, pp.328-9) on the plateau of Canayer on the Araklı Burunu headland, overlooking Hyssou Limen. The site is a rectangle measuring 200m by 300m, with a gatehouse in each wall.

... exercised the infantry there. This will have been an auxiliary cohort, perhaps the *Cohors Apuleia civium Romanorum Ysiporto* mentioned in the *Notitia Dignitatum* (*Or.* XXXVIII, 34) and by Arrian himself (as Ἀπλανοὶ πεζοί; *Ektasis* 7, 14). Arrian implies ('*As you know*') that Hadrian had personal knowledge of the unit – possibly from his tour of the area in 129 – and it is documented elsewhere (*Scriptores Historiae Augustae, Vita Hadriani* 10) that the Emperor took a keen interest in the discipline of his troops.

Although Arrian does not specify the precise nature of the exercises for the infantry and cavalry at Hyssou Limen, it may have been as much a display to show off the skills of the troops as a practical drill, like the elaborate exercises described in his slightly later *Tactics* (though of course on a much smaller scale, with only 20 cavalrymen). See *Tact.* 33-44, with A. Hyland, *Training the Roman Cavalry* (Stroud, 1993), and 10.3 below.

§2. *As Homer once said.* See *Odyssey* V.469. 'We too' is perhaps an allusion to *Od.* XII.168f.

§3-4. *Then suddenly clouds rose up* .... Although sudden storms are common in the Black Sea, Arrian's purpose in recounting his experience to the Emperor bears little relation to the 'official' strand of his letter (except, in passing, to relate the fate of one of the vessels [5.1-2 below], which Arrian evidently thought of little cause for concern). The provenance of the quoted line (*Tragicorum Graecorum Fragmenta* II.89) is unknown.

4 The treatment of the unenforced stop at the Pontic village of Athenai [87F3; now called Pazar, though it was until recently still known as Atina] is perhaps surprisingly restrained. For the most part – although the portent is signposted at 4.1 ('For there is in the Euxine Sea a place so named') – Arrian continues the story of the storm and its consequences uninterrupted right through to the end of 5. It is only then (5.3) that a specific mention is made of the co-incidence – rather, the divine providence, as Arrian suggests – that brought Arrian to this place, which happened to share its name with the scene of his correspondent's early years, and the author's own youthful studies.

§1. *There is a Greek temple ... and also an abandoned fort.* Contrary to the implication that Arrian gives at 5.3, Pontic Athenai must in fact have been more than a nameless anchorage at some point, even if it was indeed at that time deserted. Procopius (*De Bellis Justiniani* VIII.2.10) derives the name from an ancient queen of the area buried there, but it is not clear (*pace* Pekkanen [1964] p.44, following J. Jung) that this is a direct challenge to Arrian's derivation: Procopius challenges other authors' assertions that the name is derived from Athenian colonists, but of course this is not what Arrian says. But it seems that both are wrong; Bryer and Winfield (1985, pp.335-6) suggest a derivation from a Laz word meaning 'shady place'.

§2. *Aparktias ... Thraskian.* The Aparktias (or Aparkias) is the north wind; the Thraskian and Skironian come from the north-north-west (Aristotle, *Meteorologica* 363b29).

5 §3. *Timber, of which, as you know, there is a great abundance ....* Again, Hadrian's personal knowledge of the area is highlighted. The richness of the Euxine in shipbuilding materials is well documented: see Xenophon, *Anab.* VI.4.4 and Strabo XII.3.12 on timber, and Strabo XI.2.17 on wax and pitch.

6 §1. *[2]50 stades.* MS P records the distance to Apsaros as being πεντακοσίους (fifty) stades. Editors since Müller have amended this to 250, as better reflecting the true distance (computed by Müller to be 280 stades) and as being a more likely distance to be covered in the time mentioned, given the favourable weather conditions.

§1-2. *Apsaros* [87G3]. Now Gonio, in Georgia. The garrison Arrian inspected is attested not only by Pliny the Elder in his *Natural History* (VI.12), who mentions a *castellum* at the mouth of the river 'Absarrus', but also by a Hadrianic inscription from Nola (*CIL* X.1202 / *ILS* 2660), and, probably, by a papyrus found in Egypt (which, incidentally, also indicates the existence of a *canaba*, or veteran settlement, outside the fort). That *castellum* was a rectangle measuring 194m by 245m, with four gates, each having two towers, four corner towers, and five further square and three rounded towers around the perimeter; see further Levkinadze (1969) and Bryer and Winfield (1985), pp.350-1.

Although Arrian treats the fort very briefly here (and the settlement not at all, unlike that at Phasis, 9.5 below), he hints at its significance by reserving comment for the confidential, official Latin report of the inspection tour that Arrian was bound to submit. But there is no doubt that it was of great importance. This is given away by its size alone; whereas most of the forts along the Black Sea housed only single units (as at Hyssou Limen, 3.1 above, and Phasis, 9.3 below), Apsaros had as many as five, probably auxiliaries too (Speidel [1986], p.658). But a glance at its position will also hint at its significance. Not only was it located at the eastern extremity (see 11.4 below) of the Black Sea, the medium of Roman power in the region; it was also hard by the mountains that separated the Roman-controlled coastal strip from the Iberian kingdom of the hostile King Pharasmanes (see also note to 9.4 below). Indeed, the fort came into its own during the Alan invasion of 135, Arrian's repulsion of which was possibly launched from here (Speidel, loc. cit.). See also Introduction, pp.10-11.

§3. In the Argonauts legend, Apsyrtos was the brother of Medea, who killed him and scattered his body to slow down the pursuit of her father after she had fled from Colchis with Jason. Apollonius Rhodius (IV.450-81) records a slightly different version of the myth, in which Medea sets up her brother in an ambush, where he is killed by Jason. He locates the murder in the Adriatic, as does Strabo, at the Apsyrtides islands on the Pannonian coast (VII.5.5); Ovid (*Tristia* III.9) put it in Tomis. Procopius (*Bell.* VIII.2.12-14) agrees with Arrian, saying that Apsyrtos' tomb was to be found in the east of the city.

§4. Thoas was the king of Tauris, where Iphigenia became priestess to Artemis after being miraculously rescued from her father Agamemnon, who had been about to sacrifice her in order to secure favourable winds for the passage to Troy. When Orestes came to Tauris to steal its statue of Artemis, Iphigenia deceived Thoas and escaped with Orestes and the staute. Arrian is the only ancient author to suggest that Thoas died of disease.

7 Arrian breaks off from his narrative to list the geographical features he has passed along the way, in a form characteristic of the traditional *Periplus*.

§1. *Ophis* [87F4]. Listed a couple of centuries later on the source map of the Peutinger Table as the Opiunte; the name survives in the settlement of Of, at the mouth of the river, which is now called Istala Dere.

§2. *Psychros* [87F4]. Now known as Baltacı Dere.

Kalos [87F4]. Today called İyi Dere, but still apparently known as the Kalopotamos.

Rhizios [87F3]. The modern river Rize.

§3. *Askouros* [87F3]. Today, the Taşlı Dere.

Adienos [87F3]. The Peutinger Table calls it 'Ardinio'. Silberman (1995, ad loc.) identifies it with the modern Kanlü Dere, the *Barrington Atlas* and Bryer and Winfield (1985, p.332) with the Kıbledağı Dere.

Zagatis [87F3] is now the Pazar (or Susa) Dere.

The Prytanis, where Anchialos' palace is. The Prytanis [87F3] has been identified with the modern Büyük (or Furtuna) Dere. Anchialos was an important Roman vassal in the region, ruling over two tribes, the Machelones and the Heniochoi. According to Cassius Dio (LVIII.19.2), he visited Trajan at Satala before that emperor's expedition against the Parthians.

§4. *Pyxites* [87F3]. Also mentioned by Pliny (*NH* VI.12). The Pyxites is identified by the *Barrington Atlas* with the Değirmen Dere, but by Silberman (1995, ad loc.) with the Witzeh Su. Bryer and Winfield (1985), p.336, however, see in the Piskala Dere a rare (in this region) Greek survival from the Pyxites.

Archabis [87G3].   Today, still known as the Arhavi; listed as Abgabes on the Peutinger Table.

Akampsis [87G3].   Now the Çoruh, a river suggested to be important for the mineral trade that was the *raison d'être* for Trapezous itself; see Drews (1976), p.28. Procopius (VIII.2.6-9) calls it the Boas in its upper reaches.

§5. *The river Bathys* [87G3] is listed by Pliny (*NH* VI.12) as the last in the sequence of 'Acampseon', Isis, Mogrus and Bathys, and is now the Qorolistsqali in Georgia. Its harbour, Bathys Limen, is now the town of Batumi, and is translated on the Peutinger Table as Portus Altus.

Akinases ... Isis ... Mogrus [87G3].   Now the rivers Kintrish, Natanebi and Supsa respectively; the Mogrus is called the Nigrus on the Peutinger Table (and identified with the Natanebi on Bryer and Winfield's map). Note the importance Arrian evidently attaches to the navigability even of relatively minor waterways (see Introduction, p.9).

8 §1. *From there, we sailed into the Phasis* .... The Phasis river [87G2], now the Rioni, was (and remains) the most important river of Colchis, and thus central to Roman control over the interior (see Introduction, p.9). It is well documented from the earliest Greek literature, first appearing in Hesiod's *Theogony* (340), and features prominently in the geographers (Strabo XI.2.16-17, 3.4; Pliny *NH* VI.12, calling it *clarissimus Ponti*). From almost its very first appearance, the Phasis had a particular

resonance, seen as the limit of the navigable seas: Virgil lists it in his catalogue of rivers, at *Georgics* IV.367, and Apollonius Rhodius (*Argonautica* II.1261) describes it as Φᾶσίν τ᾽ εὐρὺ ῥέοντα, καὶ ἔσχατα πείρατα πόντου ('broad-flowing Phasis, and the utmost end of the sea'), a phrase echoed in a proverb recorded by Strabo that calls the river the ἔσχατος δρόμος ('uttermost course', XI.2.16; cf. also Valerius Flaccus, *Argonautica* I.2) for ships – a suitably heroic location for the Argonauts seek the Golden Fleece, and indeed for the Romans to have a fortress (see Introduction, pp.23-5). Aelius Aristides even listed it alongside the Euphrates, Ethiopia and Britain as one of the four cornerstones of the Roman frontier (*Ad Romam* 82). Significantly, Xenophon had also made a voyage to the region on the trail of the *Argo* (*Anab.* VI.2.1). The mouth of the Phasis as Arrian knew it was much wider, and further to the south, than the one we may see today; this old mouth is now the Paleostomi ('Old Mouth') lake, cut off from the sea by a low sandbar.

§2. ... *That floats 'on top of' the Peneus 'like oil'.* An apt quotation from *Iliad* II.754.

§2-5. Arrian describes the 'lightness' of the river water in comparison to the sea, first in specific connection to the Phasis, then of the Pontus more generally. He was not the first to do this: Aristotle (*Problemata* XXIII.6), Polybius (IV.42) and Strabo (I.3.4) noted this phenomenon, generally suggesting, like Arrian here, that this was because of the large number of rivers emptying into the sea, outweighing the very limited egress of water through the Bosporus into the Mediterranean. Modern theories add that when the Mediterranean waters broke into what was then a freshwater lake, about 7,500 years ago, the denser salt water sank to the bottom, leaving the lighter layer of fresher water on top (see R.D. Ballard, 'Deep Black Sea', *National Geographic* vol.199 no.5 [May 2001] 52-70).

§5. *Those who sail in ....* The Phasis was the primary
artery of transportation for Colchis: Strabo (XI.3.4) notes
that its valley was a pass into Iberia, and indeed even
today it provides a vital link for this area to the interior of
Georgia. Pliny (*NH* VI.13) records that it was navigable
by large ships for 38½ Roman miles, and even further by
small ones. As such, the fort at its mouth (see 9.3-4 below)
was particularly important (see Introduction, pp.8-9).

9 §1. *The goddess Phasiane.* Arrian identifies the local
goddess Phasiane with Rhea, herself often equated with
the Phrygian earth-goddess Cybele, whose worship was
instituted at Rome in 204 BC, and assimilated into the
official cult of the Empire by Claudius. This eastern
mystery was also often associated in Greece with that of
Demeter, whose priest Arrian was in his home town of
Nicomedia.

The one by Phidias in the Athenian Metroön. Arrian's
passing reference to this statue (the building is also
mentioned in his *Anabasis*, III.16.8) betrays a personal
knowledge of Athens perhaps gained while on Nigrinus'
consilium in c.111-14 (see Introduction, pp.3-4), and
reflects Hadrian's personal fondness for that city. The
statue is also referred to in the guidebook of Arrian's later
contemporary Pausanias, at I.3.4.

§2. Arrian's interest in the anchor of the *Argo* might be
said to reflect a typical 'Second Sophistic' preoccupation
with relics of classical Greek literature, and the fact that
the object was displayed at all reflects a similar desire in
cities across the Greek east to emphasise their links with
the glorious past (see Introduction, pp.15-16). The fact
that the anchor was fake (at least so far as Arrian was
concerned) is neither here nor there, although his concerns
might be derived from a passage (I.955-60) in Apollonius
Rhodius, in which the Argonauts' new anchor is said to be
made of stone.

§3. *In any case, the fort itself* .... Antiquarian preliminaries dispensed with, we move on to the real object of Arrian's stop at the mouth of the Phasis – the fort. The precise nature of the garrison of 400 is not entirely clear, however. στρατιῶται ἐπίλεκτοι are literally 'select troops', but often refer to auxiliary troops (e.g. Xenophon, *Anab.* III.4.3; Polybius VI.26.6-8), or more specifically to a governor's *singulares*, or personal guard of auxiliaries (see Speidel [1986], pp.659, 660 n.28; Pelham [1911], p.633), and this seems more likely than the small detachment of legionaries often proposed on the basis of the unusual presence of artillery in a frontier fort.

The safety of those who sail this way. Arrian thus identifies the primary function of the fort – presumably referring to merchant and military ships.

§4. The fortifications were unusually strong, recently (perhaps following Hadrian's visit to the Cappadocian frontier in 123/4 or 129) reinforced with walls and towers of baked brick. No trace of these survives, however, due to the silting of the river bed (see Hind [1983-4], p.92), and the fortification in any case seems partly to have reverted to wood in later antiquity (see Braund [1989], p.37, citing Agathias III.18.9). Arrian is explicit about the threat of barbarian attack and siege, and even went so far as to equip the fort with war engines – an unusual step for an auxiliary post. Quite where this threat was perceived to come from is less clear. The Alani, the usual suspects, do not quite fit here, and indeed are nowhere mentioned in the *Periplus*. Braund (1989, p.35) and Syme (1981, p.280) suggest the influence of the Iberian king Pharasmenes – to whom the nearby Zydritai are recorded as being subject (see 11.2 below) – as a possible destabilising element among the local client-kings.

§5. ... *The whole area outside the fort settled by veterans of the army, various merchants and others.* Here, as at countless sites elsewhere throughout the Empire, a thriving community of merchants and veterans attached to the fort (known as a *canaba*) had grown up outside its walls, although there is some evidence for a Greek mercantile presence – probably Milesian in origin – at the mouth of the Phasis since early classical times: a silver drinking bowl dating from the fifth century BC and inscribed (in Greek) 'I belong to Apollo the Supreme of Phasis' has been unearthed (see Burney and Lang [1971], p.224).   Strabo (XI.2.17) describes the town as the *emporium* of Colchis, and it was clearly an important staging-post for merchant ships, with such wares as ship-timber, pitch, linen, hemp and wax. (The geographer was not over-enamoured of the local honey, however, criticising it as rather bitter.) But Pliny mentions the town of Phasis (*NH* VI.13) in the past tense, and explicitly says that the only town on the river in his day (the *Natural History* was finished before AD 77) was Surium, forty miles inland: so it is possible that the town was abandoned at some point in the first century AD, only to be revived when veterans and merchants began to settle there under the aegis of the new fort at the northern end of the Cappadocian frontier.

10 Arrian switches back into the sequential list of geographical features, divided into two sub-sections – rivers and tribes – by a short account of his activities at Sebastopolis (10.3).

§1. *The navigable river Charies* [87G2]. Also recorded by Pliny (*NH* VI.14). Despite the ancient Chobos flowing to the north (see below), the modern Khobi has been identified with the Charies since the groundbreaking work of Lomouri (1957); see also Braund's note in the directory to the *Barrington Atlas* (vol.2, p.1227).

The river Chobos [87G2]. Today the Inguri, this was the river estuary in which Anicetus sought refuge after his revolt of 68/9 (see Tacitus, *Hist.* III.47-8; Josephus, *Bellum*

Judaicum II.366). Arrian's activity there – presumably diplomatic – was clearly too sensitive for a general readership, and is left in the decent (if frustrating) obscurity of the Latin report. Pliny (*NH* VI.14) reports the Chobos as flowing from the Caucasus through the territory of a tribe called the Suani.

§2. *Sigame ... Tarsouras* [87G2]. Called Sigania and Thersos by Pliny (*NH* VI.14). The Sigame must be the modern Galizga; there is a river Tanoush about 100 stades further along which may be the successor to the Tarsouras.

Astelephos [87G2]. About 150 stades from the Tanoush and the same distance south of Sukhumi (see below) is the broad estuary of the river Kodor, studded with islands; it may be that the Astelephos and Hippos were names for the two largest branches of this 'delta'. In any case, the river was significant enough to be recorded by Pliny (*NH* VI.14, as the Astelphus) and on the Peutinger Table (as the Stelippo).

§3. *We came to Sebastopolis* [87G2]. This city, on whose site stands the modern town of Sukhumi, was in Arrian's day a shadow of its former importance as a military and commercial centre. Although evidently still popularly called Dioskourias – the name of a Greek colony founded in the area that had served as Mithridates' winter headquarters in 66 BC, and by Strabo's time was a flourishing *emporium* (XI.2.16) – the city as Arrian knew it was in fact a different settlement. Pliny described the old city as deserted (*NH* VI.15), but recorded a *castellum Sebastopolis* some 30 miles distant along the coast (VI.14-16), and it seems as though this was the place that Arrian visited as part of his tour of duty in 131. The towers and walls of Roman Dioskourias have been discovered underwater (see Hind [1983/4] p.92), and it may have been the encroachment of the sea that drove its inhabitants to the safety of the *canaba* of Sebastopolis, which was on higher ground.

Arrian's visit (perhaps commemorated in an inscription found at Sebastopolis: *IAE* 1905.175; cf. Mitford [1980] p.1202), like those to Hyssou Limen and Apsaros, affords us another glimpse of the governor at work. Once again, the fort is portrayed as being in a state of readiness. The presence of cavalry, which facilitated movement in the difficult terrain beyond the immediate coastal strip, is worthy of note, and indicates that, despite the primacy of naval transport, a degree of control over the interior was necessary for the Roman presence in the area to be effective.

The horsemen leaping onto their mounts .... Horsemen leaping on to their steeds as they galloped by was the climax of the series of drills described by Arrian in the *Tactics* (43.3), and must have been an immensely difficult skill to master, not least because stirrups were as yet unknown. And difficult not only for the cavalryman; as Hyland points out (op. cit., p.159), 'it needed an honest horse to run straight knowing he was going to have over 200lb of armoured trooper thud into the saddle.' See also note to 3.1 above.

11 §1. *The Colchoi border on the Trapezuntines ....* The Colchoi, according to Herodotus (II.104-5) were of Egyptian origin, being the remnants of the army of the legendary pharaoh Sesostris. Though the term is sometimes used as a blanket name for all the tribes of the region, Arrian seems to distinguish a separate tribe of that name, and identifies them with the Sannoi, whom Pliny sees as part of the Heniochoi, *pace* Strabo, who assimilates them into the Macrones (Pliny *NH* VI.12, 29; Strabo XII.3.18). See also 7.1 above.

Drillai. The reference to Xenophon's adventures is typical. The episode to which Arrian alludes here is the

battle of February 400 BC (*Anab.* V.2.1-27), in which
Xenophon's Ten Thousand fought with the Trapezuntines
against the Drillai, a Colchian tribe.

§2. *Being pirates, they are not anxious to pay their tribute*
.... Brigandage and piracy were endemic in the region, as
noted in the Introduction (p.6), and Arrian's dark threat is
surely born more of his desire to finish the work that
Xenophon and the Ten Thousand started over five
hundred years previously, but could not finish, than of any
belief that he could purge the Black Sea of piracy. Whilst
history does not record the fate of the Sannoi, we do know
that the governor was perfectly capable of using military
might to intimidate the Caucasian tribes, as he did
against the Alani six years later.

Anchialos. See note to 7.3 above. Although Arrian does
not single out this client king for special treatment here,
he was clearly one of the more important actors on the
political stage in the region.

They are subject to Pharasmanes. Whereas Anchialos was
friendly to Rome, Pharasmanes was a different
proposition. He was king of Iberia, but his influence, as
we see here, extended across the mountains into Colchis.
See the Introduction pp.9-11 for a fuller discussion of his
rôle in the diplomacy of the period.

Lazoi. At this stage not a particularly powerful people,
by the fifth and sixth centuries the Lazoi would play a
fuller rôle in international affairs. Nothing further is
known of their king, Malassas.

§3. *Apsilai.* This tribe is mentioned by Pliny as living
north of the Astelephos (*NH* VI.14). Nothing is known of
their king, Julianus, although his name suggests that he
was a Roman citizen, and he will have received his crown
at Trajan's conference of 114.

Abaskoi. This tribe's name lives on in Abkhazia, the troubled north-western extremity of modern-day Georgia. This is their first appearance in recorded history.

The Sanigai, in whose territory Sebastopolis was founded. This phrase offers an insight into the tribal dynamics of the region. Strabo, writing under the early Principate, calls Dioskourias a Colchian city (XI.2.14); Pomponius Mela, in about AD 43, locates it in the territory of the Heniochoi (I.111). Pliny (*NH* VI.16) records that that coast is in the hands of the Melanchlaeni and Coraxi; and now Arrian has it in Sanigai country.

§4. After this list of rivers and peoples, Arrian indulges in some geographical observation, in common with a long line of authors (cf., for instance, Strabo XI.2.14; Procopius VIII.6). On the matter of the eastern limit of the Black Sea, Arrian is accurate in proposing Apsaros, *pace* Herodotus (IV.86) and Procopius (VIII.2.32, without challenging Arrian's proposal), who prefer the Phasis, and Strabo (XI.2.16), who thinks Dioskourias.

§5. *[Sailed directly towards the left ...].* The few words inserted at this point are taken from MS 1, missing as they are from P. It is easy to understand how a scribe's eye might have slipped from καταφανῶς to the κατείδομεν below it.

The Celtic Alps. Arrian's comparison of the Caucasus with the Celtic (i.e. French) Alps suggests a trip to Gaul – perhaps the same tour of duty in which he saw the rivers Inn and Save (see Introduction, p.4).

Strobilos is only mentioned by Arrian as a name for a peak in the Caucasus, and is not clearly identified from the information given here (although E.H. Bunbury has a guess at Mount Elbrouz, the highest mountain in the Caucasus, and visible from this point – *A History of*

Ancient Geography [New York, 1959 ed.], vol.2, p.512). As
the furthest extremity of the known world to the earlier
Greeks, it was only natural that it was here that
Prometheus should undergo his punishment, as recorded
by Aeschylus (*Prometheus Bound* 422, 719) and Herodotus
(I.203f., III.97, IV.12). Later, with the adventures of
Alexander, the myth was relocated to the Himalayas,
although Cicero, in his adaptation of part of the story,
returned to the Caucasus (*Tusculanae Disputationes*
II.23). Arrian cannot resist the classical allusion.

12-16. Section 2 of the Periplus *briefly covers what would
be the first portion of a conventional circumnavigation,
starting at Byzantium in the Thracian Bosporus and
sailing westwards towards Trapezous.*

12 §1. *The coast from the Thracian Bosporus as far as
Trapezous is like this.* This sentence is the only indication
we are given that this is an important point in the structure
of the work – a fact that has for some confirmed suspicions
against the authenticity of the *Periplus* (see Introduction,
pp.26-8). ἔστε ἐπί, however, is a typically Arrianic formula,
and circumstantial evidence against the aforementioned
suspicions. See also Reuss (1901), p.389.

Some editors have added a lengthy sentence between §1
and §2, which is lifted from the Anonymous *Periplus Ponti
Euxini* as it appears in MS 1 (8r38-41), and which
foreshadows and expands upon the description and
location of the Sanctuary of Zeus Ourios. In that
compilation it is used to introduce the work (after the
reproduction of Arrian's greeting to Hadrian, 1.1 above /
Anon. 8r37) and leads without interruption into 12.2,
hence the attempted editorial addition. But the excerpt in
the Anonymous *Periplus* is from Menippus, and in any
case is superfluous to the narrative of Arrian's work.

§2. *These things that I tell you, you already know.*
Although Arrian seems to imply that Hadrian had seen this
coastline for himself, it is unclear as to when he might have
done so. Certainly, neither of his two tours of the region, in
123/4 and 129, seem to have included a voyage along this
route, although we can be sure that he visited Trapezous
(see 1.1 above). This stretch of coast was, however, very
well documented, having been (unlike the rest of Arrian's
subject) part of the Graeco-Roman sphere for centuries, and
it may be that he was simply referring to the Emperor's
general erudition.

§3. *But on sailing from the Sanctuary to the right, there is
the river Rhebas* ... The reference to 'sailing to the right'
places this work firmly in the tradition of the more recent
examples of the *Periplus* genre, amongst which this anti-
clockwise direction had been predominant since
Artemidorus in the first century BC (see Baschmakoff
[1948]). The Rhebas [52E2], today the stream known as
the Riva Kalesi, is also mentioned by Apollonius Rhodius
(II.349, 650, 789) and Pliny (*NH* VI.4, giving the
alternative spelling 'Rhesus').

The Black Cape [52E2], today known as Kara Burunu,
features in Apollonius Rhodius (II.651) and on the
Peutinger Table.

Artane [52F2]. Now the Kuzgun, and also on the
Peutinger Table. Although Menippus too notes the
suitability of the mooring (5704; cf. the Anonymous *Periplus*
8r45), Arrian is the only ancient author to mention the
temple of Aphrodite – perhaps an indication of his personal
knowledge of the coast. The same can be said of the detail
included in the record of the Psilis (§4), now the Gök Su.

§4-5. *Kalpes Limen.* The harbour at Kalpe [52G2], now
Kerpe Limanı near modern-day Kefken, is easily
identifiable today from the detailed description of it given

by Xenophon (*Anab.* VI.4.3-6), who quartered his Ten Thousand on the promontory there. No wonder, then, that Arrian cites his hero by name here. It is also recorded by Pliny (*NH* VI.4); Apollonius Rhodius (II.659) and Strabo (XII.3.7) mention the river of the same name. Arrian's self-conscious reference to 'the elder Xenophon' once again indicates how strongly he identified himself with his hero: see note to 1.1 above and Introduction, p.16.

13 §1. *Rhoe* [52G2]. Now the Kumkagız Dere, emptying at Kefken.

The island of Apollonia [52G2]. Also, it seems, known in ancient times as Daphnousia, the contemporary name given in the margin of MS P and in the Anonymous *Periplus*, at 8v2-3. The Anonymous *Periplus* and Pliny (*NH* V.151) call the town Thynias; pseudo-Scylax (92) gives that name to the whole island, as does Apollonius Rhodius (II.672f.), who says that the Argonauts founded a temple to Apollo there. The island is also mentioned in Strabo (XII.3.7), and is now called Kefken Adası.

Chelai [52G2] is featured on the Peutinger Table. The Sangarios [52G3], is now the Sakarya, and mentioned by Homer (*Iliad* III.187; XVI.719) as the location of a battle between the Phrygians and the Amazons; also by Apollonius Rhodius (II.722), Strabo (XII.3.7), and Pliny (*NH* VI.4).

§2. *Hypios* [86A3]. Known today as the Büyükmelen Çayı, and shown on the Peutinger Table; see also Apollonius Rhodius II.795.

The emporium *of Lilaion* [86B2]. A staging-post for merchantmen; now the village of Akçakoca. Called Lillion in MS P and Lileon in MS v; Pliny (*NH* V.149) gives the spelling Lilaeus, agreeing with MS l (which supplies the reading given here).

Elaion [86B2]. There is a river Byleum on the Peutinger Table, perhaps corresponding to the modern river Aftun Deresı.

Kales [86B2]. Now Alaplı. See also Thucydides IV.75.2.

§3. *River Lykos* [86B2]. Mentioned on the Peutinger Table, and listed in the *Barrington Atlas* as the Gürünç Su, though Silberman (1995, ad loc.) has it as the Kilidjé Su. But it is only about 80 stades from Alaplı to Ereğli; so perhaps Pliny (*NH* VI.4) was right to situate Herakleia on the river Lykos, which would make the river the modern-day Gülüç Çay. See also Xenophon, *Anab.* VI.2.3, Apollonius Rhodius II.724.

Herakleia [86B2]. Founded in about 560 BC by the Megarians and Boeotians from Tanagra, Herakleia became one of the most important Greek cities in the region in the fifth and fourth centuries BC (for which see Jones [1971], pp.148-53, and C.M. Burstein, *Outpost of Hellenism: the emergence of Heraclea on the Black Sea* [Berkeley, 1976]); Xenophon called there on his way back to Greece (*Anab.* VI.2.1). Strabo (XII.3.6) calls it εὐλίμενος, 'well-harboured'. Its name survives today in its modern designation, Ereğli.

§3-4. *Metroön ... Posideion ... Tyndaridai ... Nymphaion.* All these places – possibly coastal shrines – remain unidentified.

§4. *Oxeinas* [86B2]. This river is probably to be identified with the Ilık Su, which flows into the Black Sea at place until recently called Oksina.

Sandarake [86B2]. Now Zonguldak, and only in fact about 70 stades along the coast.

§5. *Krenidai* [86B2]. Known today as Kilimli.

The emporion *Psylla* [86B2]. The Peutinger Table calls this trading station 'Scylleum'. The *Barrington Atlas* equates it with the modern Çatal Ağzi.

Tios [86C2]. See Strabo XII.3.8 (calling it 'Tieion'); Pliny VI.4; and Pomponius Mela I.104. Identified with Filyos (or Hisarönü); here the difficult country opens up into a wide plain between the Filyos (Yenice) and Bartın rivers.

Billaios [86C2]. Now the Filyos (or Yenice) Çayı. See also Apollonius Rhodius II.791, and Pliny, *NH* VI.4, calling it 'Billis'.

Parthenios [86C2]. Known today as the Bartın Çayı. Frequently cited in antiquity, from Homer (*Iliad* II.854) on; Apollonius Rhodius (II.936-9) makes it a favourite bathing-place of Artemis. Pliny (*NH* VI.5) also mentions it, but places it between Kytoros and Karambis (14.2-3 below). See also Xenophon, *Anab.* V.6.9 (the citation at VI.2.1 is generally regarded as spurious).

Up to here live Bithynian Thracians .... For this people, see Thucydides IV.75 and Xenophon, *Anab.* VI.4.1. The Ten Thousand split into three groups at *Anab.* VI.2.16f.; the story of their exploits before they met up again at Kalpes Limen is told at VI.3.1-26.

14 §1. *From here onwards is Paphlagonia.* Strabo (XII.3.8) agrees with Arrian on the borders of Paphlagonia and Bithynia, though Pliny (*NH* VI.5) prefers the Billaios. Mela (I.104) puts the boundary at Armene (§4 below).

The Greek city of Amastris [86C2]. Now the harbour town of Amasra. Pliny (*NH* VI.5) records its former name as being Sesamon; Strabo (XII.3.10) says that that name, of one of three towns synoecised (the other two being Kromna and Kytoros, both cited by Arrian below), is given to the acropolis of Amastris.

Erythinoi [86C2]. First mentioned in Homer (*Iliad* II.855, with Kromna and Aigialoi, below, and the river Parthenios, 13.5 above), and later in Apollonius Rhodius (II.941) and Strabo (XII.3.10), this mooring is under the headland now known as Çakraz Burunu.

Kromna [86C2]. Listed as 'Kortsch-Šile' in Silberman and Tekeönü in the *Barrington Atlas*, neither of which designations appear on Admiralty charts for the area. Pliny (*NH* VI.5) places it between the Billaios and Amastris. Also cited by Apollonius Rhodius (II.942), Strabo (XII.3.10), and Mela (I.104).

§2. *Kytoros* [86C2]. Working back from Karambis, we come to Kidros, above Sütlüce Limanı, which is the ancient Kytoros, founded by Sinope as a trading station (Jones [1971], p.148). See also *Iliad* II.855; Strabo XII.3.10; Mela I.104; Pliny, *NH* VI.5.

Aigialoi [86C2]. Now Karaagaç Limanı. Apollonius Rhodius (II.364-5, 945) and Strabo (XII.3.10) give this name to the whole shore of more than 100 stades, as well as to a village on it.

§3. *Thymena* [86D2]. Now Timne. Klimaka and Timlaion precede Thymena in the Anonymous *Periplus*, following Menippus.

Karambis [86D1]. Now Cape Kerempe. Pliny (*NH* VI.6) says that it is roughly equidistant from the Thracian and Kimmerian Bospori; Strabo (XII.3.10) points out that it is also the closest point on the Anatolian coast to the southernmost tip of the Crimea, 140 miles to the north. Also mentioned by Apollonius Rhodius (II.361-3).

Zephyrion [86D1]. To be found in the area of modern Doganyurt.

Abonouteichos [86D2]. Now Inebolu (from its later name of Ionopolis), this town was originally a Sinopean foundation, probably as a trading post (Jones [1971], p.148). Strabo (XII.3.10) seems to put it after Kinolis (below).

Aiginetes [86E2]. Now Hacıveli Burunu.

Kinolis [86E2]. Now Ginoğlu. Pliny (*NH* VI.5) calls it Cimolis, and places it (with Stephane, §4 below) just after mount Kytoros (§2 above). See also Strabo XII.3.11 and Mela I.104.

§4. *Stephane* [86E2]. Until recently this point was still called Istifan; it appears on modern charts as Usta Burunu, and on the Peutinger Table.

Potamoi [86E2]. Now under Cebelit Burunu.

Lepte Point [86E1]. Now İnce Burunu; called Syrias by Menippus (5912).

Armene [86F1]. Now Ak Limanı. Xenophon and the Ten Thousand stayed at Armene for five days (see *Anab.* VI.1.15); see also Mela I.104 with note to §1 above, and Pliny *NH* VI.6 (conflating it with Sinope, §5 below). Strabo (XII.3.10) records a proverb, ὅστις ἔργον οὐδὲν εἶχεν Ἀρμένην ἐτείχισεν, 'whoever walled Armene had no work to do'.

§5. *Sinope* [87A2]. Now the Turkish city of Sinop. Founded, possibly by Corinth rather than Miletus (*pace* Arrian and Strabo, XII.3.11), in the late eighth / early seventh century BC, primarily to exploit the mineral richness of the peoples to the east, as Drews (1976) argues, and even the Crimea. It was a significant military port under Mithridates, whose home city it was, and then under the early Empire; a fleet was still based there in

Trajan's reign, but the port seems to have declined after that.   See Bryer and Winfield (1985) pp.69-88; Reddé (1986), p.258; Boardman (1980) pp.254-5; Strabo, loc. cit., gives a lengthy description of it.

Karousa [87A3]. Now Gerze; the anchorage is sheltered by a promontory to the north. Pliny (*NH* VI.7) puts it on the other side of the Halys.

Zagora [87A3]. Hamilton (1842, vol.1, pp.301-2) equates Zagora with modern Alaçam, at the mouth of the Zalekos river, mentioned in Menippus and the Anonymous *Periplus*. But Bryer and Winfield (1985, pp.89-90) call this town Zalekon; moreoever, this site is at least 150 stades from the Halys, rather than the 30 recorded here. The *Barrington Atlas* suggests Çayağzi.

§5-**15** §1. *The river Halys* [87A3] is now the Kızıl Irmak. Arrian both indicates and exploits the great resonance the river had in ancient literature. As he notes, it was the boundary between the Persian Empire and Croesus' kingdom of Lydia (cf. Herodotus I.72), crossed by the latter in his misunderstanding of the famous Oracle (ib., I.53) that foretold a great empire's destruction. So it is entirely in character for him to point out that this great landmark of the classical Greek literary inheritance is now part of the Roman landscape (see Introduction, pp.24-5). Strabo (XII.3.9, 12) makes it the eastern boundary of Paphlagonia (cf. 14.1 above), while quoting the same passage of Herodotus as Arrian does. For the observation on the course of the Halys, cf. 11.4. Also mentioned by Xenophon at *Anab.* V.6.9; the citation at VI.2.1 is generally regarded as spurious.

§2. *Naustathmos ... Konopeion ... Eusene* [87B3]. None of these stations are identified for certain in the swampy coast to the east of the Halys.

§3. *Amisos* [87B3]. Unusual in the settlements of this stretch of coast, in that it affords easy access to the interior, Amisos is now the town of Samsun. Well attested throughout the ancient sources, it was not in fact originally a colony of the Athenians, but was founded by the Milesians at the beginning of the sixth century (though a shipment of Athenian cleruchs did arrive in 437 BC, renaming the city Peiraeus). Strabo (XII.3.14) locates it 900 stades from Sinope, as opposed to Arrian's (more accurate) 730. See Jones (1971), p.148; Boardman (1980), p.255; Bryer and Winfield (1985) pp.92-5.

The harbour at Ankon [87B3]. The Iris is now the Yeşil Irmak. See Valerius Flaccus IV.600 for Ankon, and Apollonius Rhodius II.367, Xenophon, *Anab.* V.6.9, Strabo XII.3.15, 39, and Pliny, *NH* VI.10 for the Iris.

Herakleion [87C3]. Shown on the Peutinger Table, and mentioned by Strabo (XII.3.17) and Apollonius Rhodius (II.965), this latter also in connection with the Amazons (see *Thermodon* below). Identified with the Caltı Burunu headland. Arrian almost doubles the real distance between Ankon and Herakleion.

Thermodon [87B3]. Today the Terme Suyu. The connection with the Amazons lives on even today in the nearby mountain named Masón Dagi (the ancient Amazonia; Apollonius Rhodius I.977, Pliny loc. cit.). See also Herodotus IV.110; Xenophon, *Anab.* V.6.9 (the citation at VI.2.1 is generally regarded as spurious); Apollonius Rhodius II.370-2, 970; Strabo XI.3.15; Pliny, *NH* VI.10; Arrian, *Bithynaica* frg.48 Roos; Mela I.105; and Procopius, *Bell.* VIII.2.2.

16 §1. *Beris ... Phigamous.* This sequence of rivers is not recorded in any other ancient sources (except the Anonymous *Periplus*). The Beris [87B3] is now identified with the Miliç Suyu; the Thoaris [87C3] with the Zindan

Dere; the Oinoe [87C3] with the Ünye Dere; and the
Phigamous [87C4] with the Yevis Dere, though Bryer and
Winfield's map equates the Phigamous with the Ünye.

The fort at Phadisane [87C3]. Cited by Strabo (XII.3.16)
as Phabda, and by the Peutinger Table as Pytane; the site
is now the town of Fatsa (see Hamilton [1842] vol.1, p.270;
Bryer and Winfield [1985] pp.111-12).

§2. *Polemonion* [87C3]. Formerly known as Side (Strabo
XII.3.16), the town was renamed in honour of one of the
two Polemons, kings of Cappadocia from 38-8 BC and AD
38-64 respectively. It appears also, under its new name,
in Pliny (*NH* VI.11) and the Peutinger Table. It was one
of the most important cities of this coast in classical times,
but has perhaps surprisingly never been fully excavated.
See also Jones (1971), p.170; Bryer and Winfield (1985),
pp.111-12.

Jason's Point [87C3] is not hard to identify today – it is
easily the most prominent headland on this coast and is
still known as Yasun Burunu – and provides a direct link
to the Argonauts, who are said to have disembarked there
on their voyage to Colchis, although this episode is not
mentioned by Apollonius Rhodius. Also cited at Strabo
XII.3.17; the citation at Xenophon, *Anab.* VI.2.1 is
generally regarded as spurious.

The island of the Cilicians [87C3]. Only mentioned here
and in the Anonymous *Periplus*; now Hoynat Kale.

§3. *Boön* [87C3] is listed in the *Barrington Atlas* as
Persembe, though the name Vona is still in use
(Silberman [1995] ad loc.; Bryer and Winfield [1985]
p.120). Arrian's short notice belies the fact that this is
still one of the best anchorages on the south coast of the
Black Sea.

Kotyora [87C4]. The reference to Xenophon is to *Anab.* V.5.3f.; the town is also mentioned by Strabo (XII.3.17, calling it Kytoros). The modern town of Ordu stands on or near its site.

Melanthios [87C4]. Now the Melet Irmak, and listed on the Peutinger Table. See also Pliny, *NH* VI.11.

Pharmatenos [87D4]. Identified with the Bazar (or Pazar) Suyu, but unknown from elsewhere in the ancient sources.

Pharnakeia. This settlement [87D4] is almost universally known as Kerasous in the ancient sources, and indeed is still called Giresun. The 'new' name that Arrian gives it would have been bestowed on it by the eponymous Hellenistic king who took the city in 183 BC; the remains of his fortifications can still be seen. The dual name causes confusion amongst the post-Hellenistic sources (perhaps exacerbated by the fact that the city re-adopted the old name in AD 64, as Jones [1971] p.170 says): Strabo (XII.3.17) and Pliny (*NH* VI.11) distinguish two towns – the latter placing his 'Pharnacea' opposite the island of Aria (i.e. Aretias; see §4 below), some 30 stades down the coast. Moreover, the Kerasous of the Anonymous *Periplus* (9r30) seems to match that of Xenophon (*Anab.* V.3.2), a Sinopean colony three days' march from Trapezous on the modern-day Kerason Dere, some way down the coast between Koralla and the Sacred Mount, §5 below. See Bryer and Winfield (1985) pp.126-34, 152.

§4. *Aretias* [87D4]. Pliny (*NH* VI.32) knew the island as Apollonia or Thynias, and recorded the Greek name as Aria. It also features in Apollonius Rhodius (II.1030-1230) as the Island of Ares, where the Argonauts spent a night on the way to Colchis.

Zephyrion [87D4]. The headland is now Çam Burunu; the mooring in its shelter is still called Zefre Liman.

Tripolis [87D4]. Now Tirebolu. Pliny (*NH* VI.11) mentions a *castellum* there. See Bryer and Winfield (1985) pp.138-40 for Tripolis and the *Argyria*, now the Halkavala silver mine, which was worked until about 1800, and for which Arrian (with the Anonymous *Periplus*) is the only ancient source.

§5. *Philokaleia* [87D3]. Listed on the Peutinger Table, and in Pliny (*NH* VI.11). Now the town of Görele; *Koralla* [87E3] is now Görele Burunu.

Sacred Mount [87E3]. Today still called Yoros Burunu.

Kordyle [87E3]. The town, near modern-day Akçakale, appears on the Peutinger Table; Pliny mentions a Cordule (*NH* VI.11) but places it much further to the west, around Polemonion. Silberman (1995, ad loc.) thinks it may be a different feature of the same name, for which see the Anonymous *Periplus* 9r39.

§6. *Hermonassa* [87E3]. The mooring at Hermonassa, now Akçaabat, is so good that, until recently, it was used as a bad weather alternative for Trapezous itself (Bryer and Winfield [1985] p.160). See Strabo XII.3.17.

There you are building a harbour .... Traces of an ancient harbour wall, now submerged, known as the Molos may reasonably be assumed to be the remains of Hadrian's harbour (Bryer and Winfield [1985] p.180).

17-25. The third and final section of the Periplus
*completes the circuit of the Black Sea after the retrospective
of 12-16, picking up the narrative where it was left at
Sebastopolis and continuing round to Byzantium.*

17 §2. *The voyage sailing to the right from Byzantium....*
A formula typical of the *Periplus* tradition; see note to 12.3
above.

§3. There is no suggestion here that Arrian actually
undertook the voyage around the coasts subsequently
described for the benefit of his Emperor – indeed, that is
implicit in several remarks in the text, principally the
description of Leuke, 21-23 below, which he says 'are
reports from those who have either landed there, or have
learned it from others' (23.3). Again, the dimensions of
the Maiotis lake given at 19.3 are acknowledged to be
second hand. This is in marked contrast to the first eleven
chapters, in which it is absolutely clear that Arrian had
personally visited the locations described.

Kotys, king of the so-called Kimmerian Bosporus ....
Although not under the direct control of Roman troops
(their last outpost being, as Arrian notes, the fort at
Dioskourias), the Bosporan Kingdom (centred on what is
now the Crimea and the north coast of the Sea of Asov)
was a key part of the complex network of client kingdoms
by which Rome maintained its influence in its frontier
regions. Kotys II, who reigned from AD 123/4 until his
death in late 131 (which, of course, gives a date for the
Periplus; see also Introduction, p.35 n.12) was one of
these client kings: a Roman citizen (Ti. Julius Cotys) who
called himself φιλόκαισαρ φιλορωμαῖος – a friend of Caesar
and of Rome. The continuation of Roman influence in the
kingdom was of vital importance to Rome – not only
because of the Bosporan corn supply, but because of the
activities of barbarian tribes in the area who had the
potential to threaten the Roman presence along the

Danube and in Dacia – and so Arrian's expectation that
Hadrian would want to monitor the situation closely was
probably well-founded (and in fact mirrors the similar
decision of Corbulo to send Nero a map of the area
recorded in Pliny, *NH* VI.40). In the event, Kotys'
successor (Ti. Julius) Rhoemetalkes I, who was to rule
until 153/4, dedicated a statue and an inscription to
Hadrian at his accession, and seems to have been as
assiduous a friend of Rome as his father.

18 §1. *Pityous* [87F1]. Now Pitzunda, in Georgia, and
mentioned by Strabo (XI.2.14). According to Pliny, the
town in his day was deserted, having been sacked by the
Heniochoi (*NH* VI.16). A Roman garrison was later stationed
there, in the second half of the second century AD.

§1-2. *Nitike, where a Scythian tribe used to live of old.*
The Anonymous *Periplus* calls this place Stennitike (9v44;
though in such a context – εἰς Στεννιτικὴν χώραν – to make
it probable that this is a corruption, i.e. of εἰς τὴν Νιτικὴν).
Nitike [87F1] is otherwise unrecorded in the ancient
sources, but would, on Arrian's description, equate roughly
with the modern region of Gagra. The Scythian pine-cone
eating tribe gets somewhat more exposure, firstly (as
Arrian says) in Herodotus (IV.109), and later in Strabo
(XI.2.1), Mela (I.110) and Pliny (*NH* VI.14), who places
them between the Charies and the Chobos rivers (10.1
above).

§2. *Abaskos* [87F1]. This river, not mentioned outside
Arrian or the Anonymous *Periplus*, clearly derives its
name from the Abaskoi tribe, already mentioned at 11.3
above, in whose territory it flowed. It is now probably the
Lapsta.

Borgys [87F1]. Unlocated, but mentioned by Ptolemy
(V.8) under the name Brouchon, echoing the name of a
tribe (the Brouchoi) in Procopius (*Bell.* VIII.4.1) that

occupied the territory between the Abaskoi and the Alanoi.

The Nesis ... where Herakleion Point is. Herakleion Point [87E1] is probably Cape Adler – about the only geographic feature on this coast which matches Arrian's narrative. The river that flows into the sea at Adler, which would be the Nesis, is the Mzynta.

§3. *Masaïtike* [87E1]. Only mentioned here and in the Anonymous *Periplus*. Now Matsesta, in Russia.

Achaious [87E1]. Also featured on the Peutinger Table, and to be equated with the river of the Achaei mentioned in Pliny (*NH* VI.17): now the Sochi river. Arrian has it as the southern boundary of the territory of the Zilchoi, a people well attested in various locations in the north east corner of the Black Sea (see Strabo XI.2.12, 14, calling them Zigoi; Pliny, *NH* VI.19, as the Zigae; Procopius, *Bell.* VIII.4.1-2, as the Zechoi) and whose movement throughout the six hundred years represented by these citations is symptomatic of the fluidity of population movements on the frontiers of the Empire. At this point Stachemphax, king of the Zilchoi, is clearly part of the client king network that ran along the whole east coast, but nothing else is known of him.

Herakleia Point ... the point which is a shelter .... If we take Arrian's distance from Achaious to Herakleia as correct, these two promontories become very difficult to identify, as this stretch of coast is not rich in headlands. The first headland north of Sochi is Mys Uch-Dere, but it is only about 70 stades from Sochi; there are a couple of higher points of land at 150 stades, but they are slightly inland. The second point should fall just north of what is now Lazarevskoye, but the same problem arises here, too. But working back from Pagra Limen, below, which is easily identified, we find two headlands at the correct

distances which fit the bill. I therefore propose that the
southern point of the two, Herakleia, is the headland now
known as Mys Kodosh, sheltering Tuapse, and the more
northerly, anonymous one is Mys Gryaznova – making the
distance from Achaious to Herakleia more in the region of
500 stades.

§4. *Palaia Lazike ... Palaia Achaia* [84E4]. These two
names ('palaia' meaning 'old') again highlight the extent of
tribal movements in the region. The Lazoi, as recorded
above (11.2), resided by Arrian's day further south,
between the Zydritai and the Apsilai: and the Achaians,
mentioned by Strabo (XI.2.14) though not by Arrian, have
left further traces in the Achaious river already recorded
in §3 above, 600 stades to the south. Numerous attempts
have been made to equate these names with modern ones;
it seems that they denote general areas formerly occupied
by these tribes, more or less around the modern
anchorages of Tenginskaya and Vulan respectively.

Pagra Limen [84D4]. Not otherwise attested; now
probably the harbour at Gelendzhik.

Sacred Harbour. This might be Pliny's Hiero (*NH*
VI.17), and a possible alternative name for the port of
Bata (also mentioned by Strabo, XI.2.14). Now the
harbour of Novorossisk.

Sindike [inset, 87L2]. Strabo has a 'Sindic harbour and
city' (XI.2.14) 180 stades east of the Bosporus, but this
would appear to be too close to match Arrian's Sindike – a
term Strabo applies to the whole region, with a capital at
Gorgippia (today's Anapa; see Gorbunova [1971/2] p.58,
Hind [1992/3] p.108), 'near the sea' (XI.2.10), which may
be more likely. See also Mela I.111 (as Sindos); Pliny, *NH*
VI.17.

19 §1. *Pantikapaion* [ins.84K2] was the most important town of the Bosporan Kingdom, and was described in detail by Strabo (VII.4.4). It is now the town of Kerch', in the Ukraine. See also Boardman (1962/3) pp.45-7 and (1980) p.253; Gorbunova (1971/2) pp.53-4; and Hind (1992/3) pp.102-3.

The river Tanaïs, which is said to divide Europe from Asia. Adherents of this view, that the Tanaïs – now the Don – was the boundary between the two continents include ps-Scylax (68), Strabo (VII.4.5; XI.2.1), and, by implication, Pliny (*NH* VI.18, locating the Maiotis Lake, now the Sea of Asov, in Europe). Arrian does not express a preference between the Tanaïs and the Phasis, either here or in his discussion of the latter (8.1-5 above). Herodotus (IV.45) preferred the Phasis, though he did record the claim of the Tanaïs too. It will also be noted that Arrian errs about the course of the river, and was not the only ancient author to do so; see also Strabo II.4.6.

§2. *Aeschylus, however, in* Prometheus Unbound .... The play from which these lines (*Trag. Gr. Frag.* III.190) come is, of course, lost. Procopius (*Bell.* VIII.6.15) also refers to this passage, and indicates that it comes from the very beginning of the play.

§3. *It is said that the circumnavigation* .... Arrian here indicates to us that he is using a source, and has not himself been to the Maiotis lake; see note to 17.3 above. Strabo also quotes the figure of 9,000 stades (II.5.23); Polybius is nearer the mark with 8,000 (IV.39.1). Neither is quite so far out as Pliny, however, who almost doubles the size of the lake at *NH* IV.78, giving 1,406 Roman miles as the circumference.

Kazeka [ins.87J2]. Some ruins near the modern village of Katschik, on a salt lake connected in ancient times to

the sea, may be the site of this town, which is mentioned
only here and in the Anonymous *Periplus*.

§3-4. *Theodosia* [ins.87I2].   This town (whose name
survives in that of the modern city of Feodosiya) was
founded in the early sixth century BC (see Boardman
[1980] p.252), and is cited by, amongst others, Strabo
(VII.4.4, as the boundary of the Taurians and the
Bosporans), Mela (II.3), and Pliny (*NH* IV.86). There is no
other evidence to suggest that it was deserted at the time
Arrian was writing, however – and, moreover, plenty
(archaeological and literary) showing that it was a
flourishing town in the first century AD and into the fourth.
It has been suggested that Arrian here was using a source
going back to the destruction of the time of Mithridates;
perhaps more probable is the suggestion (for which see
Patsch (1904) p.74) that this was a more or less temporary
abandonment following a barbarian raid (but see also the
note on the mouths of the Ister at 20.3 below). Arrian does,
after all, provide plenty of evidence for increased activity in
the area by the tribes of the Scythian hinterland.

§4. *The deserted harbour of the Skythotaurians* [23H4].
This strange-sounding amalgam of peoples is first attested
in Pliny (*NH* IV.85): they first settled in this area in the
third century BC. After Mithridates, the Skythotaurians
were nominally under Bosporan rule, but the level of
integration was still evidently low.   The Anonymous
Periplus (12r18; 12v5) names their harbour as Athenaion,
possibly following Menippus; today, it is known as Sudak.
The cause for its reported desertion is, like that of
Theodosia, unknown, though it may well be due to the
same factors, or even (as Silberman [1995, ad loc.]
suggests) struggles between the Scythotaurians and their
supposed Bosporan overlords.

Tauric Lampas [23H4] is not attested elsewhere, apart
from in the Anonymous *Periplus*. It is now Biyuk-Lambat.

§5. *Symbolos harbour* [23G4]. Also mentioned by Strabo (VII.4.2) and Pliny (*NH* IV.86); the Anonymous *Periplus*, after Menippus, calls it Eubolos. The site is on what is now the bay of Balaklava.

The Tauric Cherronesos [23G3]. Cherronesos (more usually spelt Chersonesos) was an important city, founded by Megarians from Pontic Herakleia (see 13.3 above) in 422/1 BC, and as such is well recorded in the ancient sources (including Pliny, *NH* IV.85; Strabo VII.4.2-3; and Mela II.3, who spells it as Arrian does and attributes its foundation to Diana). Its remains are near Gurtschi, a village in the region of Sebastopol. See Boardman (1962/3) pp.44-5 and (1980) pp.251-2; Gorbunova (1971/2) pp.52-3; Hind (1992/3) pp.97-9.

Kerkinitis [23G3]. The principal archaeological site on what is now known as Karkinitskiy Bay is near modern-day Kalancak, and corresponds to the descriptions of the ancient site given by, among others, Herodotus (IV.55), Pliny (Carcine, *NH* IV.84), and Mela (II.4). But Arrian's Kerkinitis matches another site further south, in the next bay, near Eupatoria (Yevpatoriya) (for which see Boardman [1962/3] p.44 and [1980] p.251; Hind [1992/3] pp.96-7); and whether there were two towns known by the same name, or Arrian (or his source) is simply confusing the two, is unknown. This must also be the same harbour as described by Strabo (VII.4.2), although he leaves it anonymous.

Kalos Limen [23F3]. Settled from Chersonesos in about 300 BC, but apparently abandoned in the mid-first century AD; now Chernomorskoye. See also Mela II.3; Boardman (1962/3) p.44; and Hind (1992/3) p.96.

20 §1. *Tamyrake* [23G3]. This corresponds to the long strip of land known to antiquity also as 'Achilles' Racetrack' (Δρόμον Ἀχιλλέως – see e.g. Mela II.5, Pliny,

NH IV.83) – a name which Arrian mistakenly gives as an alternative to Achilles' Island, or Leuke, in 21 below – and now called Tendra, though Strabo gives the name only to the eastern tip (VII.3.19) or as an alternative for his 'Karkinites' Bay. See Hind (1992/3), p.96.

Eion [23G3]. This must be Tendrovskiy point, the very tip of Tendra, from which the mouth of the Borysthenes is about 150 stades directly across Yegorlystskiy Bay.

Borysthenes [23F2].   Now the Dnieper.   Arrian's measurements seem to indicate that he used this term to represent the broad estuary of the Dnieper, often called Hylaeum Mare in antiquity, as an integral part of the river.

§2. *Olbia* [23E2].   Now the town of Parutino, on the lower Bug (ancient Hypanis), Strabo (VII.3.17) and Pliny (*NH* IV.82) knew it also as Borysthenes; Strabo also records that it was founded by the Milesians. There was a Roman presence in the town from the mid-first century AD, and an established garrison by the reign of Antoninus Pius.   See also Herodotus (IV.18); Mela (II.6); Minns, 'Thirty years of work at Olbia', *JHS* 65 (1945) pp.109-112; Boardman (1962/3) pp.42-3 and (1980) p.251; Gorbunova (1971/2) p.50; and Hind (1992/3) pp.94-5.

A small island, deserted and nameless.... This island is Berezan, and was settled in very early times by Greek colonists, though it appears the town did not survive very long (see Boardman [1980] p.250).   An inscription to Achilles dating from the end of the first or beginning of the second century AD has been found there (Gorbunova [1971/2] p.49).   See also Boardman (1962/3) p.42; Hind (1992/3) pp.92-4. It is also anonymous in Strabo (VII.3.17, 19), but Mela (II.98) and Pliny (*NH* IV.83, 93) both equate it with Leuke and the Isle of Achilles, which Arrian comes on to in 21 below.

Odessos [23F2]. Here we reach the first Odessos of the *Periplus* (for the other, see 24.4 below), cited also by Pliny (*NH* IV.82), who calls it Ordesus. No known site matches Arrian's description, though what may be its location is in fact back at the mouth of the Dniepr, where a site has been excavated near modern Ochakov. See Boardman (1962/3) p.42.

The harbour of the Istrians [23F2], only mentioned in the Anonymous *Periplus* (13v20) apart from here, is probably around Kujalnik, and may be the modern Luzanovka. It is now the bay shown on Admiralty charts as Port Yuzhnyy, at the mouth of which is Grigor'yevka.

§3. *The harbour of the Isiakoi* [23D2]. Again only in the Anonymous *Periplus* (13v22). Now Odessa.

The mouth of the Ister called Psilon. The Ister is now, of course, the Danube, and here Arrian comes to its marshy delta, now in Romania. Ancient sources disagreed on the number of mouths of the Ister, much as they did on the same question with regard to the Nile. Arrian plumps for five – along with Herodotus (IV.47) and Ephorus (quoted in Strabo, VII.3.15) – a figure he also cites in his *Anabasis* (I.3.2) and *Indica* (II.15). Pliny (IV.79) went for six; but the traditional number was seven (see in particular Strabo, loc. cit., Ovid, *Tristia* II.189, Statius, *Silvae* V.2.137, Valerius Flaccus IV.718 and VIII.187, and Tacitus, *Germania* 1; Mela II.98 says there are six islands *inter Histri ostia*, implying seven mouths). It will be noticed that adherents of the 'five' are an older tradition – another reason for thinking (along with the desertion of Theodosia, 19.3-4 above, and the omission of Tyras, below) that Arrian's sources may be somewhat old for this stretch of the coast.

The stretch between is deserted and nameless. Arrian, not for the first time in this part of the *Periplus*, is mistaken; and this is probably his most serious error. The city of Tyras, known to Strabo (VII.3.16), and situated on the river of the same name, had gone through some troubled times in its history, but by the end of the first century AD was once more a flourishing city. It is unlikely that Arrian would have ignored it, even if it had been temporarily abandoned, as Stadter (1980, pp.39-40) suggests: he mentions such cities elsewhere (e.g. the harbour of the Skythotaurians, 19.4 above, or Bizone, 24.3 below). Is there a *lacuna* in the text, or was Arrian simply let down (as perhaps seems more likely) by a combination of poor sources and careless compilation?

21 1. *An island, which some call Achilles' Island ....* The first and last names given here are widely attested for a sacred island in these parts, to be identified on Arrian's (and indeed Strabo's, at VII.3.16) description of its location with what is now Zmeinyi island (or Serpilor, in Romanian): the second name, 'Achilles' Racetrack', should actually refer to Tamyrake (20.1 above). However, many ancient authorities (such as Pliny, *NH* IV.83, and Mela II.98) give these names to the modern-day Berezan, which Arrian recorded as 'deserted and nameless' (20.2 above). The fact is that dedications to Achilles have been found on both islands (see note to §2 below for the Zmeinyi inscriptions), and there is no trace of a temple, a common feature of many of the descriptions in the ancient sources (see Gorbunova (1971/2), p.49; Hind (1992/3) p.91; also Pausanias, III.19.11), on either.

Whatever the details and precise locations, it is clear that the north west corner of the Black Sea had a strong association with Achilles, and this was expressed in a cult of Achilles 'Pontarchos' centred on Olbia. The legends out of which this cult grew date from the eighth century BC, and there is evidence of the cult itself from the fourth century; see the article by Dzikowski in *JHS* 59 (1939), pp.84f.

It is said that Thetis set it up for her son .... There is an alternative tradition that the hero's tomb was on Leuke (see Pliny, *NH* IV.83, X.78; Euripides, *Andromache* 1259-62). Philostratus (*Heroicus* 54.6) also records an alternative version of the legend concerning the creation of the island, that Thetis asked Poseidon to raise it as a refuge for sailors. There is a thread of this theme of help to sailors in distress in the version of Arrian – see 22.2 and 23.1-2 below.

§2. *Inscriptions, some in Latin, some in Greek* .... See L. Robert, *Hellenica* XI-XII p.274 for the few inscriptions which have been found on Zmeinyi.

§3. *For those who wish to pray to Achilles also honour Patroclus along with him.* The dual cult arrangement, by which a sacrifice to one dedicatee of the sanctuary also honours the other, mirrors that set up by Hadrian to Hermes and Philesios at Trapezous, noted by Arrian at 2.2 above.

§4. *These birds attend to the temple of Achilles.* For birds in the service of Achilles on Leuke, see also Pliny, *NH* X.78.

22 §2. *Whereas others are forced to land by a storm* .... See note to 21.1 above for a version of the legend that makes Leuke's primary purpose a refuge for sailors.

§3. *For there is an oracle in the temple* .... As the island is uninhabited (21.2 above), it is unclear what sort of oracle this should be – even natural oracles, like the one at Dodona, needed human interpretation.

The victim then stands there of its own accord. It was of course a requirement of any animal sacrifice that the animal should be a willing victim; this was usually achieved by stunning the beast with the butt of an axe.

For a discussion of the sacrifices on the island of Leuke, with some interesting parallels in Russian peasant religious rites of the 1920s, see J. Tolstoi, 'Un miracle d'Achille dans l'Ile Blanche', *Revue Archéologique* 26 (1927), pp.201-6.

23 §1. *And others say that Achilles has appeared to them ... on their sail ....* The comparison with the Dioskouroi is apt; there was a cult of the Dioskouroi centred on the Greek cities of the west coast of the Black Sea, particularly in Tomis.

§2. *They also say that they see Patroclus ....* This fact is not mentioned in any of the other extant accounts of Leuke, and hints at the significance of Patroclus for Arrian and, more particularly, for Hadrian. See note to §4 below.

§3. *These things that I have recorded ....* Again, a second-hand report. See note to 17.3 above.

§4. *The love and friendship because of which he wanted to die after his beloved.* Arrian here touchingly and subtly compares the intense grief of Hadrian following the death of his favourite Antinous in Egypt in 130 – only a year or two before – to that of Achilles for Patroclus, calling to mind the hero's words at *Iliad* XVIII.98-9, αὐτίκα τεθναίην, ἐπεὶ οὐκ ἄρα μέλλον ἑταίρῳ κτεινομένῳ ἐπαμῦναι ('I would die immediately, since I could not save my slaughtered comrade'). Together with the implication that the double shrine of Achilles and Patroclus on Leuke mirrored the quasi-divinification of Antinous which Hadrian was affecting at that moment, Arrian's description of this sacred island offers his friend some comfort, as well as casting the Emperor in an heroic, Homeric light.

24 §1-2. *From the mouth of the Ister called Psilon ....* Arrian picks up the traditional *Periplus*-form narrative for the last time, from where it was left at 20.3 above (see note). He names only three of the five mouths of the Ister that he distinguishes, whereas Ammianus Marcellinus names all of his seven – in reverse order (in relation to Arrian): Peuce, Naracustoma, Calostoma (incidentally, the branch used by the Argonauts to escape from the Colchians, Apollonius Rhodius IV.303-6), Pseudostoma, Borionstoma, Stenostoma, and Septimum. Pliny (*NH* IV.79) gives 'Sacer' as an alternative for Peuce, and omits Septimum; the Anonymous *Periplus* (14v9-10) also calls it Hieron, or 'Sacred', and perhaps this survives today in the dedication of the southernmost branch to St George. That aside, there is little point in trying to marry up the branches identified in antiquity with what we see in the marshy delta today, altered even further than it may otherwise have been by the requirements of heavy shipping that use this still-important waterway.

The city of Istria [22F4]. See Mela II.22 (calling it Histropolis); Herodotus (II.33), Strabo (VII.6.1) and Pliny, *NH* IV.44 (all claiming it as a colony of Miletus). Boardman (1962/3) pp.37-39 and (1980) pp.247-9 describes in detail significant finds from the site, now Istere; see also Hind (1992/3) pp.89-90.

Tomis [22F4], now the important Romanian port of Constanţa, is perhaps the most famous of the Greek colonies of the west coast of the Black Sea, due to its most reluctant resident, Ovid. Mela (II.22) calls it Tomoe, and Pliny (*NH* IV.44) Tomos; the MS for Arrian also give several different forms of the name apparently derived from 'Tomea' or 'Tomeis' – variations not attested elsewhere. Strabo (VII.6.1) puts the town 300 stades south of Istria. See also Boardman (1980) p.247; Hind (1992/3) p.89.

§3. *Kallatis* [22F5]. Now the resort of Mangalia. Strabo (VII.6.1) records it as a colony of the Herakleotai, but Mela

(II.22) claims it for the Milesians; Pliny (*NH* IV.44) gives an old name of Cerbatis. See also Boardman (1962/3) p.35; Hind (1992/3) pp.88-9.

The harbour of the Karians [22F5]. This will be in the shelter of Nos Shabla, Bulgaria. Pliny (*NH* VI.20) records that the Karians were the first to colonise the north-east corner of the Black Sea. See also Mela II.22.

Tetrisias [22F5]. Now the Nos Kaliakra headland. Mela (II.22) calls it Tiristis; it is recorded on the Peutinger Table as Trissa. Strabo (VII.6.1) mentions a Cape Tirizis, but does not locate it precisely. See Hind (1992/3) p.87.

Bizone [22F5] was originally founded on the Charakman promonotory, near modern-day Kavarna, where remains can still be seen. But it was destroyed in an earthquake in around 50 BC, and was later rebuilt in a different spot. It is mentioned by Pliny (*NH* IV.44), Mela (II.22) and Strabo (VII.6.1 and I.3.10); see also Hind (1992/3) p.87.

§4. *Dionysopolis* [22F5]. Now Balchik. Known to Strabo (VII.6.1) as Krounoi; Pliny (*NH* IV.44) gives the old name as Crunos, but Mela (II.22) distinguishes two towns. See Hind (1992/3) p.87.

Odessos [22E5]. Originally a Milesian trading colony, dating from about 570 BC, Odessos (now Varna) later founded Dionysopolis/Krounoi and Bizone, and became a Roman city in about 27 BC. It is cited by Pliny (*NH* IV.45), Strabo (VII.6.1) and Mela (II.22); there is a full discussion in Boardman (1980) p.247, Hoddinott (1975) pp.49-56, and Hind (1992/3) p.87.

The foothills of Haimos [22C6]. The Haimos ridge, now Stara Planina or the Great Balkan, extends right out to the Black Sea coast, culminating in the headland known as Nos Emine or Cape Ermine. See also Pliny, *NH* IV.45; Strabo VII.6.1.

§5. *Mesembria* [22E6]. On the borders of the provinces of Moesia and Thrace; now Nesebur. As a Megarian colony (as Strabo says, VII.6.1) of the late sixth century, the town quickly became a rival to Apollonia (below). See also Herodotus IV.93; Mela II.22; Pliny, *NH* IV.45; Hodinnott (1975) pp.41-9; Boardman (1980) p.247; Hind (1992/3) pp.86-7.

Apollonia [22E6]. Situated on the island of St Kiriak and the Sozopol peninsula, 180 stades straight across the bay of Burgas. The town was founded in the late seventh century by Milesian colonists, and became important enough itself in the next two centuries to settle Anchialos (now Pomorie, above). Strabo (VII.6.1) claims the city as a Milesian colony, and records the distance between Kallatis (§3 above) and Apollonia as 1,300 stades, to Arrian's accumulated 1,340. See also Herodotus IV.90, 93; Mela II.22; Pliny, *NH* IV.45, recording a former name of Anthium, and 92; Hodinnott (1975) pp.33-41; Boardman (1980) pp.246-7; Hind (1992/3) pp.84-5.

§6. *Cherronesos* [22E6]. Not cited by any other ancient authors, except the Anonymous *Periplus* (15v27). Listed in the *Barrington Atlas* as Maslen Nos, but the site may lie a bit further north, between Nos Kolokita and Nos Korakya.

Aulaiouteichos [22E6]. Again, only cited in the Anonymous *Periplus* (15v29), apart from here. Now known as Akhtopol, from its later name Agathopolis.

Thynias Point [52C1]. Now Koru Burunu, above Igneada, Turkey. Cited at Strabo VII.6.1 and Mela II.23; Pliny (*NH* IV.45) records a town of this name.

25 §1-2. *Salmydessos* [52C1].   Now Midye.   For Xenophon's dealings with Seuthes the Thracian, see *Anab.* VII, *passim*; for Salmydessos, see op. cit., VII.5.12-13. Strabo (VII.6.1) backs Arrian up, describing Salmydessos as ἔρημος αἰγιαλὸς καὶ λιθώδης, ἀλίμενος, ἀναπεπταμένος πολὺς πρὸς τοὺς βορέας, 'a desert and stony beach, harbourless and wide open to the north winds', and warning of a plundering Thracian tribe named the Astoi who attack those who beach there.   Mela (II.23) and Pliny (*NH* IV.45) call it Halmydesos.

§3. *Phrygia*.   Probably the Kara Burunu headland, 330 stades from Midye.

The Kyaneai [53B2] are a group of rocks once reputed to clash together, crushing passing ships between them, with the added danger of being of varying position.   That notwithstanding,   the   *Argo*   passed   through   them unscathed, with the help of Athena (Homer, *Od.* XI.62-79; Apollonius   Rhodius   II.317-40,   549-618).   Cited   by Herodotus   (IV.85)   as   the   place   from   where   Darius marvelled at the Euxine; also by Mela (II.99), Strabo (I.2.10,   III.2.12,   VII.6.1),   and   Pliny   (*NH*   IV.92),   some under the alternative name of the Symplegades.   Both names are given by Hyginus, *Fab.* 20.   Strabo (VII.6.1) makes 1,500 stades to be the distance from Apollonia (above) to the Kyaneai, to Arrian's 1,280.

§4. *Sanctuary of Zeus Ourios* [53B2].   Arrian has already mentioned this at 12.2 above; although he has been narrating down from the European coast to Byzantium he has included these two landmarks (including Daphne, below, now Umuryeri) on the Asian side of the Bosporus before   returning   to   Byzantium   to   complete   the circumnavigation.

Maps

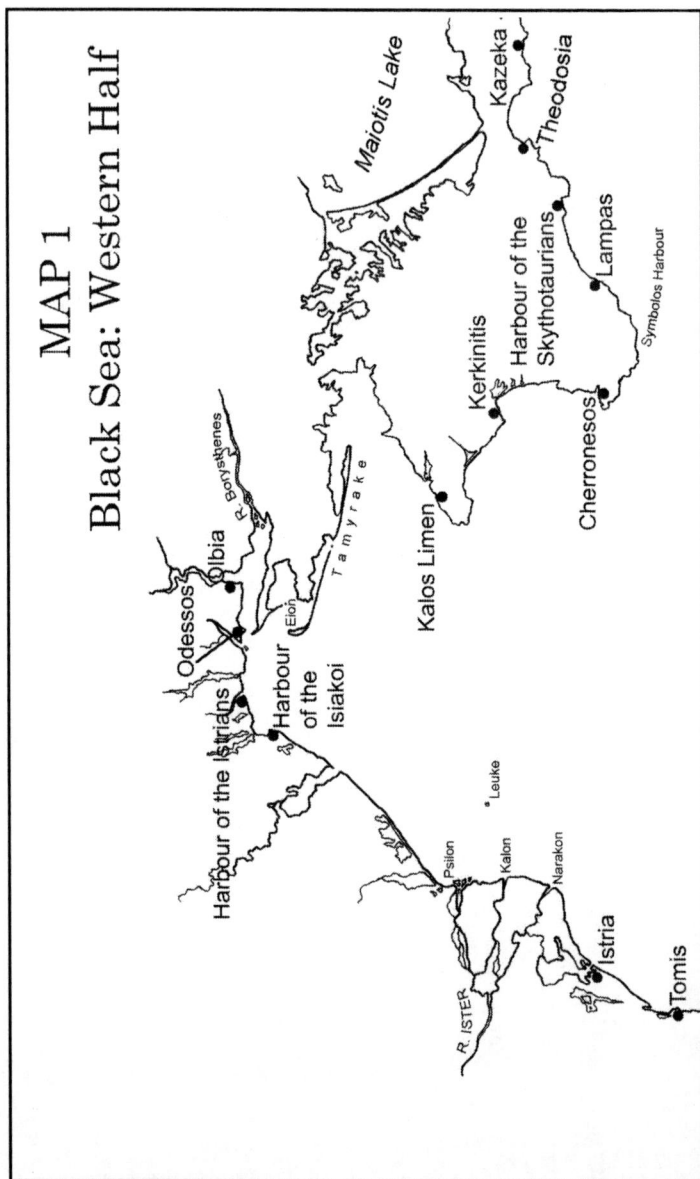

MAP 1
Black Sea: Western Half

Town

Scale c. 1 cm : 300 stades / 60 km / 38 miles

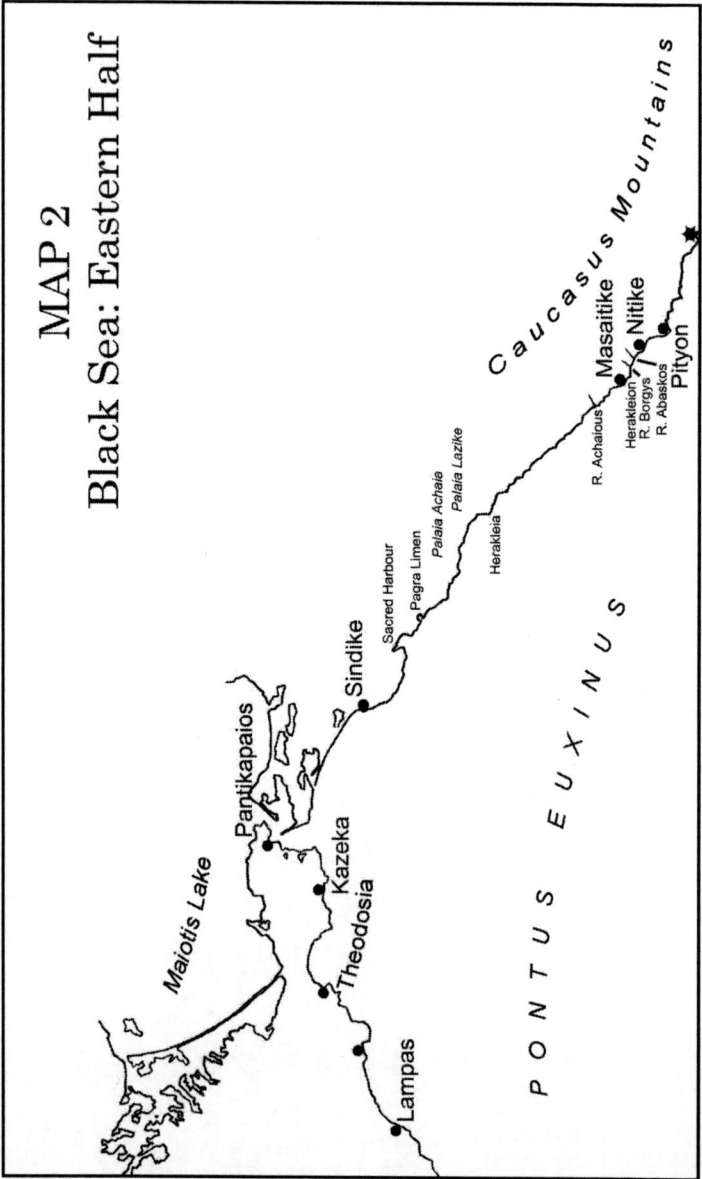

MAP 2
Black Sea: Eastern Half

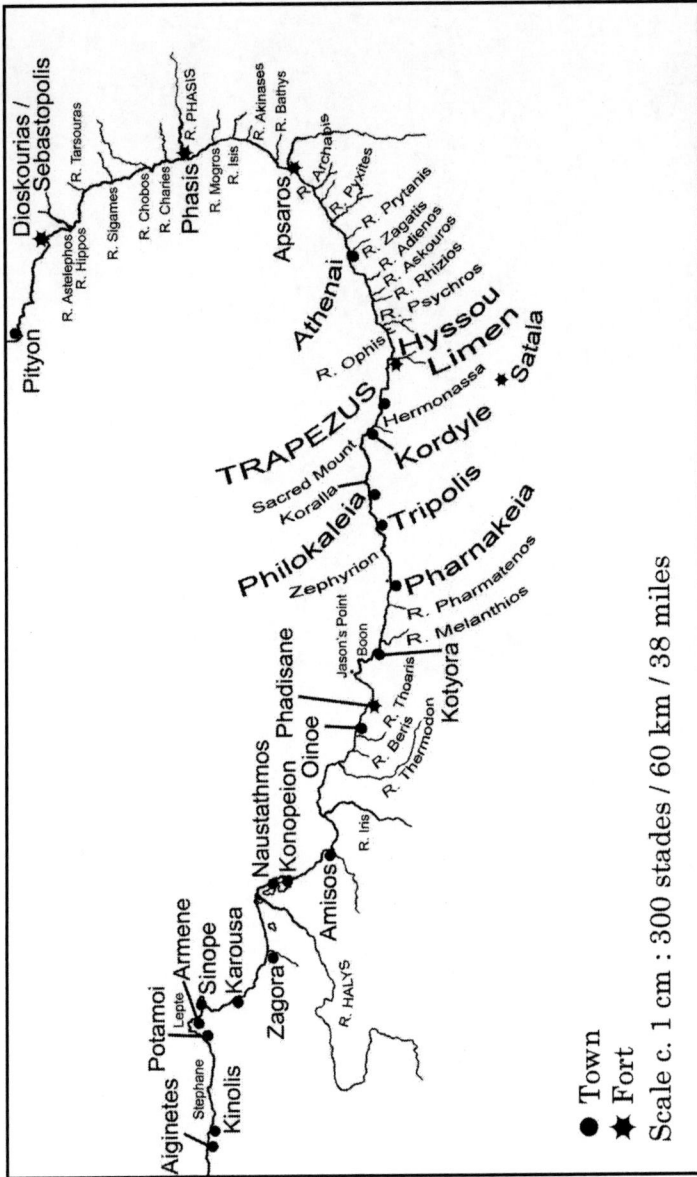